WILL

104 DAYS OF MY SON'S LIFE

TO

THAT GIVES THE GIFT OF LIVING

LIV

ANGELA LEE

Will to Liv Press

Copyright © 2025 by Angela Lee Jenkins

All rights reserved.

No part of this book may be reproduced or transmitted in any form or by any means, electronic or mechanical, including photocopying, recording, or by any information storage and retrieval system, without prior written permission of the publisher, except in the case of brief quotations embodied in critical articles and reviews.

This book is a work of personal experience and reflection. While based on real events, some details have been changed to protect privacy. The author is not a medical or mental health professional, and this book is not intended as a substitute for professional care.

Published by Will to Liv Press

ISBN (Paperback): 978-1-7642726-0-5

ISBN (eBook): 978-1-7642726-1-2

Printed in the United States and Australia by print on demand services (Amazon KDP and IngramSpark)

Dedication

For my children, Will and Liv.
And for the circle of women by my side — I am because we are.

Preface

I never thought I'd write a book. Writing was never on my vision board — and neither was this journey. None of it was. I never imagined myself here, telling this story. But sometimes purpose chooses you.

When my son Will was born, his life was short — just 104 days. He didn't get the chance to build his own legacy. So, this book is my way of giving his life meaning beyond those days in hospital. It's his story, and it's mine too, all weaved together.

Will's message deserves to be out in the world. Once it's here, it will live on forever, creating ripples I may never see but that I know will matter.

This isn't the book I planned to write, but it's the one I get to. And if you've ever lost, loved, wondered how to keep going — or simply wanted to live more fully — I hope it reminds you, as Will reminded me, that the *will to liv* is always inside us.

Angela

Contents

PART ONE: THE STORY   1

  1. The Mexican Babymoon   2
     'A sliding doors moment'

  2. The Pregnancy   13
     'Where there is life there is hope'

  3. Will Jenkins   30
     'Where there's a Will, there's a way'

    3.1 Welcome Will – The Miracle Baby   30
    3.2 The Early Days   38
    3.3 We're Gonna Love You Like We're Gonna Lose You   40
    3.4 The Will to Fight   49
    3.5 Goodbye Will   65

  4. The Maze of Grief   75
     'Life breaks everyone, it's who can put back the pieces'

PART TWO: THE HEALING   106

  5. The Ripple Effect of Trauma   107
     'Post-traumatic stress or post-traumatic growth'

6. For Better but Not for Worse   121
    'Every little thing gonna be alright'

7. The Light of Liv   123
    'My rainbow baby'

8. Coming Home   139
    'The will to liv starts now...'

Appendix: The #104Will Challenges   155
Appendix: 104 Commitments   161
Acknowledgements   168
About the Author   170

PART ONE

THE STORY

CHAPTER 1

The Mexican Babymoon

"A Sliding Doors Moment"

Babymoon time. Playa Del Carmen, Mexico—here we come. Some moments don't seem significant until you look back and realise, they changed everything. This would become one of those.

We were finally there. I never would have imagined it would take three years—three long, gruelling years of trying, hoping, heartbreak, and relentless persistence—to go on a babymoon. And yet, here we were. Craig and I were off to Mexico to celebrate his ten years at his company with free flights and what was meant to be our last holiday together before the baby arrived.

But instead of celebration, the trip began with tension and a fight.

I was up at the ridiculous hour of 3 a.m., already irritable and exhausted, driving an hour to Craig's work to pick him up straight off a night shift before heading to the airport. It was hardly the recipe for a relaxing holiday. I was furious that Craig had waited so long to book our free flights—forcing us onto this ridiculous early departure—and even more frustrated that we'd only managed to secure premium economy because business class was fully booked.

Yes, I was annoyed at our free premium economy flights. How on earth I could be annoyed at something like that I don't know. I mean how selfish. It sounds so trivial and shallow, but I can't simply blame it on pregnancy hormones. The resentment had been building long before this trip.

It started at nine weeks pregnant—the day Craig, without a word to me, bought himself a Mercedes AMG sports car. While I was busy planning budgets, restructuring my business to become more child-friendly, and obsessing over every detail in preparation for our baby, he made an extravagant impulse purchase. It wasn't about the money; (I came to realise), it was the betrayal, the secrecy of going behind my back while I carried our child. I felt it in every fibre of my being. The visceral reaction I had to it was so intense it actually made me physically sick.

I tried to rationalize it as a mini midlife crisis—after all, Craig was 43 and about to become a first-time father. I'd heard stories of other men making a "last big purchase" before their babies arrived, and friends had told me it sometimes took a year for husbands to come to terms with fatherhood. But deep down, I knew it was more—a message I'd chosen to ignore: if you don't start listening to those whispers, they come and hit you on the head.

Craig, meanwhile, was exhausted from his shift and increasingly frustrated with what he saw as my ingratitude. I can't speak for him, but I felt the weight of his annoyance. Before I got pregnant, I was incredibly self-sufficient—an achiever, a multitasker, who just handled stuff without needing help. But pregnancy changed everything. Suddenly, I really felt I needed Craig. I needed him to share the load, to help plan for the baby, and to support me in ways I'd never required before.

And I started to voice it, a far cry from my old self who would much prefer just to keep the peace. Perhaps he felt I was taking the focus off him, or that I'd changed too much. (But aren't you meant to change when you become a parent?? Surely just a bit). In our ten years together, we rarely fought—maybe just a small tiff here and there—but this was different. I saw sides of Craig I'd never known, and maybe he saw a side of me that he hadn't either. I tried to chalk it up to the stresses of becoming first-time parents, but the tension was real.

Yet, the trip had to go on. That was my motto. I was once the determined Angela who set a goal and achieved it—relentless, type-A, willing to try every natural, alternative, even "woo woo" therapy before eventually moving on to IUI cycles and IVF.

To be fair, both of us had faced years of challenges trying to fall pregnant. We started with the hopeful mantra, "it will happen when it's meant to," and then six months, and then 12 months passed by while we questioned what was wrong. Despite being 34 and 40 and seemingly healthy and fit, doubts crept in. I began to notice, wherever I went, pregnant women who were overweight, unfit—unhealthy, even. I hated the judgmental thoughts that followed, yet they fuelled my frustration and the angry energy that I knew couldn't help anyone fall pregnant.

My quest for a baby led me deep into research on hormones, hormonal balance, and stress management. I dove into yoga, embraced "really" clean eating, and started countless gratitude journals, daily meditations, and affirmations—pages filled with declarations like, "It is my intention to have a healthy, happy pregnancy and baby" and "I am so grateful for the opportunity to bring this baby into the world." I clung to these affirmations as though they could change my biology, even as my desire to have this baby consumed every thought.

I was surprised by the intensity of that desire—so intense, so all-consuming. For a woman who had always prided herself on achieving goals, the inability to conceive made me feel like a failure. I took on all the blame, convinced it was solely my fault, even though I'm sure Craig's age and sperm count could have been part of our struggles. I'm not sure why women are made to bear the burden of blame for a lot of fertility challenges or maybe I was just blaming myself and even if Craig had tried to ease that burden, I never felt it.

I continued trying. I moved on to energy work, acupuncture, naturopathy, herbs, and supplements—but nothing worked. Eventually, scans with an advanced imaging specialist revealed I might have endometriosis. I'd experienced heavy, painful periods before, but this was different. After a discussion with my obstetrician, we decided on laparoscopic surgery. In hindsight, I'm grateful we did it, because the surgery revealed severe endometriosis and sluggish fallopian tubes—issues that needed immediate attention. We were told that our best chance to conceive was within six months of the surgery, before the condition could worsen. After a few months of trying naturally, we moved on to IUI cycles. I remember literally calling Craig off the golf course so we could rush to the clinic, where, right before ovulation, his sperm was injected in the hope it would survive the journey. Month after month passed without success.

When it seemed, there was no other option, we turned to IVF—a method I strongly resisted as I wanted to conceive as nature intended. Should we force something that was meant to happen naturally? If I couldn't conceive with Craig, did that mean our future was not meant to be? The thought crossed my mind, fleeting and horrifying. But then I looked to friends who had achieved their dreams through IVF, and a conversation with a friend who had twins reassured me: at school parties and functions, no one cared how you conceived. What mattered was the family you built. So, finally, after all the resistance and doubt, I embarked on the IVF journey.

It wasn't an easy path. The medication made me feel bloated, altered my moods, and left my body feeling foreign. I nervously awaited daily updates from the IVF lab on what was happening with Craig's sperm and my eggs in that sterile petri dish. Every day was an exercise in hope and anxiety, waiting to hear if an embryo would form and survive the crucial five-day window before being implanted back into me. And then, on our first attempt, we were fortunate—a single embryo made it to five days and was implanted. The next stage was a nerve-wracking wait until the embryo reached 12 weeks. At nine weeks, during an obstetrician visit, we finally heard little Will's heartbeat for the very first time, and by 12 weeks, we received the all-clear. Phew… we did it! Our little boy was on the way, and after three years of one hell of a ride our dream was coming true.

But then, as fate would have it, while enroute to our Mexican babymoon, the universe decided to remind us that nothing was ever simple. We had a stopover in LA, and it was there that I began noticing a peculiar pressure in my stomach. It wasn't severe—just an unsettling sensation. I wondered, "Is this normal? Is it because the baby is growing now that we're 15 weeks in?" I brushed it off as nothing more than the discomfort of not being able to elevate my feet in business class—a decision that did not sit well with me. Craig, the eternal fixer, swung between frustration at my worry and forced optimism, assuring me that everything would be fine while conveniently ignoring the problem. I didn't know then that this pattern of dismissal and worry would only intensify in the months and years to come.

After over 20 hours of sharing uneasy silence and digs at each other during our journey, we finally touched down in Cancun. The early evening air was heavy and warm—hot in that unmistakable holiday way, with high 20s and a touch of humidity. The airport buzzed with life, filled with holidaymakers arriving for their own escapes. It was exactly what we needed—a reminder that we were somewhere new, somewhere full of possibility. Our mood shifted, if only slightly, as we tried to leave our tensions behind and embrace the promise of the holiday.

We set off on a drive to Playa Del Carmen, marvelling at the enormous five- and six-star resorts along the way. We checked into a villa right on the beach—a picture-perfect retreat that seemed almost too good to be true. I couldn't help but think that if I set the intention hard enough, I could control the outcome and make this trip amazing. *(Apparently, I believed I had that power.)*

After a jet-lagged sleep and a leisurely breakfast, we finally settled on the beach for some much-needed downtime. It was relaxing couple time at last—nothing to do, nowhere to be, just the sound of the waves and the growing life inside me. I gazed out at the white, white sand and the crystal-clear, sparkling blue ocean, the sunlight reflecting off the water in a way that made everything seem magical. It was a postcard view. I thought it was amazing. Craig, however, couldn't understand why we'd fly 20 hours to get here when some of the world's most beautiful beaches were only minutes from home. Fair point, I suppose—but I was an explorer at heart. I thrived on new places, fresh experiences, and adventures that nourished my soul. For Craig, home was where his routines lay, and in his mind, this trip was a favour he was doing for me. I knew it was—and in many ways, I was grateful.

The resort was filled with people from many different countries, and with pregnant women everywhere at various stages of their journeys. It was comforting to see so many others embracing the beauty and struggle of pregnancy. I lost myself in a self-development book while Craig relaxed into a Jeremy Clarkson book. He'd laugh quietly, then refuse to explain what was so funny—because, apparently, I would find it offensive. In the bits he did share, he was right. He had never shared those types of views before. It was quite an odd feeling, and I remember being slightly confused by it. We had been together 10 years, and I had no idea he agreed with some of those, what I would call 'old school' beliefs. And to be honest he probably had no idea about some of mine.

And there I was, busy staging the standard bikini baby bump shot for my imminent Facebook announcement about my pregnancy. You've got to get the right angle, the right collage of pictures and then try to come up with one of the most original, witty Facebook pregnancy announcements. I wasn't even sure if I was seeking validation from the world or connection from my husband. In hindsight, perhaps both.

As the day heated up, I needed a break from the sun and some of my thoughts that were going around in my head. I headed back for a nap, desperate for alone time a moment of calm. Craig, as was often the case, wandered off to find some golf to watch on a resort TV—oblivious, or perhaps purposefully detached from all that was consuming me. Little did either of us know, one of the biggest, most life-defining moments of our lives was waiting just around the corner.

I awoke from my restful nap and made my way to the bathroom. That's when I saw it—bright red, fresh blood on the toilet paper. In that instant, my heart began to race, and my stomach dropped. A thousand butterflies filled my chest as I raced to the balcony and called out for Craig. Called out multiple times that is to get him away from the golf. I hurried back to the bed, lying down and focusing on my breathing, drawing on years of yoga and meditation. I kept telling myself, "Everything is fine. So many women experience bleeds during their pregnancies and go on to have healthy babies." But deep down, something was wrong.

We needed a plan. Here we were, in Mexico—the other side of the world—with our growing child who had taken three years to conceive. Craig arrived back to the room and in that critical moment, he called the hotel reception for a doctor. Before long, the doctor and his assistant arrived. Amidst a maze of thoughts about whether my travel insurance would cover an incident like this (I'd only recently switched to a pregnancy-friendly plan), I found myself questioning everything.

Am I having a miscarriage? Everything is totally fine? Am I going to lose the baby? Am I going to have to go a Mexican hospital? Do they have proper hospitals? Breathe Angela, this is nothing. Does this Dr know what he is doing? Stop worrying Angela this is fine. The Dr has worked in Sydney. Universe, please give me a sign if this is something I need to worry about?

I repeated these questions silently, trying to steady myself. The doctor, speaking in reasonably good English, assessed me and insisted that I remain lying down. Then, without warning, he called for an ambulance. In what still seems like a surreal dream, I was soon being stretchered out of the villa into an ambulance. Part of me sensed the gravity of the situation, while another part tried to see the humour in it that this would someday make for an eventful holiday story—the kind where, despite the drama, everything turns out fine. I have had plenty of those stories and surely this was one of those.

We arrived at the hospital, and thank God, it was clean, modern, and far from the third-world facility I'd dreaded. We were quickly taken to a private room—a space that felt both clinical and intimate. First came the ultrasound. Lying on the exam table, time slowed to a crawl. I squeezed Craig's hand so tightly my knuckles turned white as I waited for that scan. Every moment was drenched in fear and hope.

Then, I heard it—the heartbeat. Strong, steady, and so desperately reassuring. Relief washed over all my body, and I allowed myself to cry. But then came the next part: the doctor examined my cervix and remarked, almost clinically, "You nearly had an abortion." I knew he meant miscarriage—a word that struck me like lightning. I'd been so focused on the scan, so fixated on that tiny heartbeat, that I barely noticed the blood pooling on the exam table until his words forced me to confront it. The fear returned in full force.

Craig immediately got through to our obstetrician back home. His calm measured voice on the phone became a lifeline: "Bleeds happen. Get some rest. No sudden movements." Even as his reassurance echoed around me, so many questions and doubts swirled in my mind.

That night, after long, intense discussions about what to do next—was it safe to stay? To fly back? —we decided to return to the hotel. We would rest for a couple of days before catching an earlier flight back, with a stopover in LA to break up the journey and hopefully let things settle.

We will never know if this decision was the right decision. You can never predict the future, and you never get to take a decision back. I have replayed this decision over and over and over and over. Did I really want to leave or was I pleasing Craig who wanted to leave? Was I worried about the health insurance not covering us and that was the reason? Should I have had more confidence in the Mexican Doctor and not made judgements? Or was I just being an optimist thinking that everything would be fine so there was no need to stay? The questions become never ending and there really is no point to them. I know what is done is done. I totally get that. Making peace with this decision and other decisions however is just not an easy thing to do. Just when you think you have, you haven't.

For the next 24 hours, I remained almost immobile—only walking the few meters needed for breakfast or a brief stroll to the beach—while Craig tried to salvage the holiday with his unwavering optimism. He wanted to explore, to try more restaurants, to insist that everything would be fine. I, however, was cautious. I noticed more discharge, and after hours spent messaging friends, Googling, and reading blogs, I was told that such discharge was "very common in pregnancy." Craig helped by researching too, assuring me that everything was going to be okay. Yet, deep within, a small, persistent voice wondered if this might be something more after going down a rabbit hole reading about premature rupture of membranes. Surely, that couldn't be me. Waters break just before labour, not at fifteen weeks, right?

Somehow, we made it back home. Ironically, we flew business class on our return, with a two-day stopover in LA at an airport hotel, before heading straight to my obstetrician—who promptly sent us for another scan.

That scan was our sliding doors moment. And as we sat there, waiting for the results, we had no idea what was ahead.

CHAPTER 2

The Pregnancy

"Where There Is Life, There Is Hope"

Just three weeks ago, we were so excited looking at our healthy baby on the 12-week scan. I remember how clearly we could see our tiny little bubba floating, arms and legs moving freely in the amniotic fluid. It was a perfect moment—one of the happiest of my life. But that day now felt like a distant dream.

Today's scan was a different story. The screen was blurry. I stared hard, willing myself to find something that resembled a baby. The technician's face changed, and I knew. She didn't need to say anything.

Later, they told me it was PROM—premature rupture of membranes. My waters had broken.

At first, I didn't understand what that meant. I just knew something was wrong. Amniotic fluid is what helps cushion the baby, what allows them to move, and most importantly at this stage, it's what helps their lungs develop. I couldn't see the baby clearly anymore on the scan—not because they weren't there, but because there was barely any fluid to see them in.

I was in shock, trying to hold back the tears and remain positive that this was only a little setback. I was taking big deep breaths, letting out even bigger sighs when the news became so overwhelming I broke down in tears. I was too distraught to walk out the clinic and we were quietly led out the back entrance—away from the happy couples in the waiting room. I remember thinking, how is this my story? How did we go from everything looking so good to this?

Our next stop was the obstetrician—James. I trusted him deeply. He had been with us through everything: my endometriosis surgery, the IUI cycles that didn't work, and then finally the miracle of our IVF success. James was calm, methodical, and honest. He explained that there was no way to patch the rupture. Some in-vitro studies were exploring options, but there was no safe or proven treatment. The fluid was leaking out, and we couldn't stop it.

There was so much to take in at that appointment. James laid it all out with his usual calmness, but the words were brutal.

I was told to prepare for the likelihood that I'd go into labour soon. They called it a "late miscarriage." I was told to expect bleeding. That most women in my situation deliver within a week of their waters breaking.

The chances of me having this baby alive were extremely slim. And even if the baby survived, we were looking at a high likelihood of serious disabilities—physical, neurological, or both.

They couldn't tell if the lungs were developing. Apparently, the only way to know would be at birth. Either the baby would breathe… or they wouldn't. There was no scan, no measurement, no reassurance. Just time. And breath. And chance.

Then James paused. He looked at me—not as a doctor, but as a human—and said gently: We have options to terminate now as this pregnancy was not meant to be or the other way to look at is: "Where there is life, there is hope."

Those words landed in my body so strongly then and as they do now. They felt truer than anything I'd heard so far. Not scientific. Not strategic. Just true.

I grabbed onto that sentence like a lifeline. I didn't need graphs or percentages. I needed something to hold onto that wouldn't break.

There was life. Our baby had a heartbeat. A strong one. That meant we had hope.

And for me, there was no decision to make after that. I didn't know if I'd ever get another chance to carry a child. This was our only successful embryo. The road to get here had already been long, exhausting, and emotional. But I knew in my heart—if there was even the smallest window, I would walk through it.

Decision made.

To be honest, I truly believed things would work out. Friends of mine had rocky pregnancies. I'd heard their stories. I figured this was just our version of that. A bumpy start on the way to something beautiful.

From here, my instructions were clear: rest, wait, pray we made it to 24 weeks.

That was the viability line—the point where doctors might try to save our baby. Technically, there were some success stories from 22 weeks, but 24 was the benchmark. If we could just get there... we had a chance.

Nine long weeks away.

Of course, just as all of this was happening, I was meant to be running a major work retreat. Because... of course I was. And of course, I still tried to. From the couch. From bed. From a reclining camp chair on the verandah with my legs in the air and a laptop balanced awkwardly on my belly.

As a business owner, I was used to delivering—no matter what. And I did. I pulled it off. I organised schedules, supported presenters, and made it work, even if it was from a distance. But looking back, I wonder... was it resilience, or was it avoidance? Was I listening to what my body—and my baby—really needed?

One of the areas I'd been teaching others about was stress management. Lifestyle interventions. Nervous system regulation. And now I was the one applying it all to myself. Meditation. Journaling. Breathwork. Gratitude lists. You name it, I did it.

Well... almost all of it.

The one thing I hadn't quite mastered was self-love. Particularly the kind that sets boundaries. The kind that says you don't have to prove your worth by performing while your world is falling apart. That lesson would take me a long time to unpack.

Slowly, the shock of those first few weeks began to settle. There was no more Mexico babymoon. No "normal" pregnancy experience. Just stillness and survival. After even more research and back-and-forths with specialists, I made the decision: I was going on full bedrest until this baby was born and in my arms.

Although they couldn't confirm the sex, they thought it was a boy.
But I already knew.
I knew this was Will.

Doing nothing sounds easy. Until it's all you're allowed to do.

I had exercised nearly every day of my adult life. I was always on the move—setting goals, building programs, ticking things off. My identity was wrapped in being active, productive, useful. And now? I was being asked to lie down. For days. Weeks. Possibly months.

It broke me in a different way.

I tried to keep some sense of normalcy. My days were spent rotating between the bed, the couch, and the verandah recliner where I could get sun and fresh air. I drank litres of water to help amniotic fluid production. Craig—ever the engineer—kept topping up my bottles, reminding me that if I drank enough, the baby might wee more... and we could generate new fluid that way.

That was the plan:
Drink water → baby wees → fluid builds → lungs develop.
Simple. Except we couldn't plug the rupture. The fluid just kept leaking out.

So, I tracked the leaks obsessively. Every colour, every pad, every hour. Some days it was clear. Some days pink. Sometimes nothing—which was just as stressful. Did that mean the baby was finally absorbing some? Or was there nothing left?

And the mental spiral began.

Did I eat too many hot chips in the first trimester?
Was it the two walks I did up Mt. Coolum and Mt. Ngungun?
Was it stopping the progesterone early because it made me nauseous?
Was it the retreat? The stress? The IVF itself?
Maybe my body just wasn't meant to do this. Maybe I wasn't built to carry life.

I knew those thoughts weren't helpful, but they still came. On repeat. For 85 days.

And yet, in between the spirals, I found some sanity. I created a bedrest-friendly workout with a stretchy band and music. Nothing fancy—just something to keep my mind engaged and my body moving ever so slightly. But even that made me feel guilty. Should I have just rested more? Was I diverting energy away from the baby to protect myself?

Everything became a question. Every movement a calculation. Every moment a mix of hope, fear, and guilt.

The next part of the plan was trying to keep the amniotic fluid in. I tried everything—legs up the wall, different positions, barely engaging my core. I held in every cough, every sneeze, even laughter. I was scared to move, in case it made things worse.

And still, it never made sense.

Some days, I could walk to the kitchen and barely leak. Other nights, I'd wake up drenched despite lying still for hours. It was maddening. I had to wear pads constantly—monitoring every colour, every drop. Trying to decode whether it meant something good or something terrifying.

It wasn't just exhausting—it was mentally punishing. Because even when I was doing everything right, things still leaked. Still felt uncertain. And the worst part was... I couldn't know what was helping and what wasn't. All I could do was keep going.

Craig and I researched everything. We were in deep—reading studies, following forums, reaching for anything that might help. Bone broths. Collagen supplements. If they could help repair a gut lining, maybe they could help heal the amniotic sac. There were even in-vitro studies that hinted at it. It was a long shot, but everything was on the table.

I was the kind of person who believed I could control things. That if I just did enough—thought the right thoughts, ate the right food, took the right supplements—I could fix it. Thoughts create our reality, right? I had to believe that.

So, I visualised. I wrote intentions. I repeated affirmations. I filled journals with gratitude. I stared at the vision boards I'd made long before this pregnancy—covered in images of happy, healthy kids. Surely that meant something. Surely this baby would be okay. My baby had to be okay.

Once a week, I got to leave the house for my alternating appointments—one week to the imaging clinic for a scan, the next to see James and talk through the results. It became my version of getting out. I started to feel like my Grandma (love you gma) —who genuinely looked forward to her medical appointments. When you're housebound for weeks, even a scan can feel like an event.

Every appointment was the same rhythm. We could never see the baby properly on the scan—just a blurry outline in the absence of fluid. And each time, they offered us the option to terminate. But every week, our baby was still growing. Still within normal range. Still a strong heartbeat. Still here.

At 22 weeks, Craig and I drove to Brisbane to meet a leading specialist. We wanted to make sure we had all the information before we crossed that threshold—because once we reached 24 weeks, termination would no longer be a legal option.

That appointment was tough.

We were told the "take-home baby" rate for our situation was less than 10%. I didn't even know that was a thing—a "take-home baby rate." It meant our baby might survive for a short time in intensive care... but never come home. And of that 10%, only 30% might be healthy. The remaining 70% would likely have moderate to severe physical or intellectual disabilities.

Not exactly reassuring odds.

Termination was still on the table. But it wasn't what I had imagined. I assumed it would be a gentle caesarean under anaesthetic. It wasn't. We were told we had two choices:

Be injected with something that would stop the baby's heart, then deliver

Or be induced to deliver the baby naturally, where it would die because it was too young to breathe

I remember feeling stunned. These were the kinds of conversations no one prepares you for. They were so clinical. So final. So unimaginable.

On the long drive home, stuck in peak-hour traffic, Craig and I talked. We went over and over every option. Every possibility. Every heartbreak. But in the end, two things were clear for me:

I truly believed I could handle whatever happened. We're not given anything we can't handle.

If my baby was still fighting, still growing, still showing up—I would fight too. With everything I had.

Did I really understand what that meant at the time? Probably not. But I believed it with my whole heart.

And besides, I still believed my baby was going to be fine. Healthy. Coming home. So, I didn't really need to worry about those stats… right?

We were so close to that 24-week milestone—just a couple of weeks to go. I kept repeating to myself: You can do this. We've got this.

And then, at 23 weeks and 4 days, it happened.

Another bleed. This one heavier than the one I'd had at 20 weeks. I was admitted for monitoring at our local hospital. Given steroids—to help boost the baby's lungs in case he came early. They really thought he might be coming.

I was placed in an ambulance and sent straight back to Brisbane. The local hospital didn't have the neonatal support or high-risk monitoring I now needed. A midwife rode beside me. Craig followed behind in the car.

I was scared.

More than scared—I was frightened. Not just for what was happening… but for what was coming. What if the baby came now? What if I gave birth in the ambulance? Would he be alive when we got there?

I closed my eyes, silently cried, and focused on one thing: my breath.
Just breathe. In and out. Get to the hospital. That's all you have to do.

I had no idea that I wouldn't see my home again for nearly five months.

—

Somewhere amid the ambulance rides, hospital monitors and hard conversations, there was also this beautiful news: my sister Kristy gave birth to her first baby—a healthy, perfect little girl named Rosie May.

A few months earlier, we'd been glowing sisters, excited to be pregnant together. Dreaming about raising our babies side by side. Our mum—finally about to become a grandmother after all her friends already had—was absolutely buzzing. It felt like such a special chapter for our family.

But then things changed. While Kristy prepared to give birth, I was confined to the couch, barely able to move, living in the unknown—unsure whether my baby would live or die. And Kristy, being the beautiful soul she is, kept showing up. Positive. Gentle. Empathetic. I can only imagine how hard that must've been for her—carrying the weight of her own first-time-mum fears, while watching her sister navigate every possible complication.

She held it together so well. Until one day—just a week before Rosie was born—we both couldn't anymore. She came to visit me at home, and as we hugged goodbye, something broke open. We both burst into tears and just held each other. There were no words—just this shared, aching release. Looking back, I think she must've carried so much fear into that birth.

And then, of course, comes the strange emotional dance of celebration and caution. All you want to do as a new mum is talk about your baby. Show them off. Share every detail. And I wanted Kristy to have all of that. I really did. She deserved it. And yet, I could see how mindful she was of me. How her joy came with a quiet shadow of guilt. Even though none of this was her fault, she still carried that. It's funny how we work, isn't it? How we hold guilt over things that aren't ours to carry.

Kristy has always been incredibly empathetic. And I could feel what she was experiencing without her needing to say a word.

Rosie May was such a gift. Nursing her, holding her, was helping me get through. A reminder of what I was fighting for. That this pain, this fear, this whole journey—it was all leading to something. That one day, I'd be holding my baby too.

—

Arriving at the hospital in Brisbane was intense. This was an emergency situation, and within hours of getting there, I was already being monitored and met by what felt like a new team of people—each with more statistics, more warnings, more options. I was read a list of risks for babies born this prematurely after PROM. I didn't want to hear them. I didn't care.

My answer was clear: Yes. Do everything you can to save my baby.

I signed the forms—resuscitation, ventilation, a magnesium flush. I didn't hesitate.

The magnesium flush was a tricky one. It could help protect the baby's brain—but it only worked if given within 24 hours of birth. And you only got one shot. If they gave it too soon, and he didn't come, we'd miss the window. But if we waited too long, we might miss it altogether. It was a gamble no parent should ever have to consider.

I was also visited by a hospital priest. He stood by my bedside and gently offered to say some prayers. And while there was something comforting about his presence, it also shook me. You don't send in the priest unless the situation is truly life or death. And suddenly, that was no longer an abstract possibility—it was the air I was breathing.

Thankfully, our baby didn't come that night. I was moved to a hospital room for further monitoring.

Hospital life was… surreal. The beds. The smells. The routine. The food—which, honestly, wasn't bad. But the whole environment felt foreign. I didn't feel like I belonged. I was a health professional. I believed in the wellness model, in preventative care, in movement and natural healing. Yet here I was, attached to monitors, being jabbed for blood tests every couple of days, with cannulas constantly going in and out of my arms.

I've always been someone who faints during blood tests. But now I was having so many, the nurses were running out of veins to use. I told myself to harden up. This was my initiation. I was about to become a mum.

As part of my hospital stay, I was taken on a tour of the NICU. It was confronting. I was wheeled in and shown a premature baby in a humidicrib—so tiny, translucent almost. I could barely comprehend that what I was looking at was a human. Everything about it was so small, so fragile. How could something that delicate ever grow into a child, let alone an adult?

I'm glad I saw it. It helped prepare me, at least mentally, for what could come. But I also detached. That wouldn't be my baby. My baby would hold on. My baby would be bigger. My baby would come later.

—

And then… we made it.
24 weeks.

We had crossed the line. A "viable" baby. It sounds so clinical, but in the eyes of medicine and the law, it was the day our foetus officially became a baby.

Up until now, only close friends, family, and some work contacts knew I was pregnant. I hadn't made a public announcement. I hadn't posted a bump photo or shared the news on any social media. Part of me hadn't wanted to. Not while everything was so uncertain.

But when we hit 24 weeks, something shifted.

I was pregnant with my first child. Why shouldn't I celebrate that?
So, I did.

I posted a picture of myself in my hospital bed, 24 weeks pregnant. I made it a positive post, carefully leaving out the traumatic details of the past three months. I focused on the joy. On the fight. On the hope.

A part of me believed that by announcing it, I was claiming the outcome. That it would lead to a happy ending. And honestly? The outpouring of love and support I received gave me the energy to keep going. Every message, every, "you've got this" helped carry me through.

—

As things settled and I was deemed stable, we consulted with the hospital team and made the decision to move into the apartments across the road. They were literally attached to the hospital. A lot of high-risk patients did it. It gave us a little more space, a little less stress, and I could still wheel over for appointments and monitoring.

Looking back... I think I did most of the "consulting." I think I needed to feel like I had some control.

But in hindsight, it probably wasn't the best move.

Within two weeks, I was back and forth with more scares—more stints in the birthing suite. One time, the baby's heart rate dipped dangerously low. They thought it might be time. The magnesium flush was ordered.

For the next 12 hours, I lay there, being monitored, Mum and Craig at my side, trying to help me stay calm and not have a baby. Easier said than done.

Relaxing while receiving high-dose magnesium is... next level. The flushes came in waves—hot, forceful, overwhelming. I could feel them surging through my body like fire. My biceps and forehead veins bulged like an angry bodybuilder on steroids. Then came the nausea. The dry heaving. The dizziness. I told myself maybe this was some kind of pre-labour initiation—prepping me for what was to come.

But yet again—another false alarm.

This little baby was still hanging in there. Still growing, though he had now dropped to the low end of the growth charts. Another week passed. Another round in the birthing suite. I was becoming an expert at not giving birth.

And somehow, I was calm. I knew in my bones he wasn't coming yet. Not this time.

And yes, in the middle of all this, I was still working.

Taking calls. Joining Skype meetings. Trying to support my team and hold the business together. I convinced myself it was healthy—something to keep my mind occupied. But looking back now? I was obsessed. I was clinging to work like it was a lifeline, as if staying productive proved I was still capable. That I wasn't failing. That something—anything—was still functioning.

I don't know why I cared so much. Maybe because everything else was falling apart. My body was breaking down. My whole world was uncertain. And work was the one thing that still gave me a sense of usefulness.

And part of me believed: They'd do the same for me…?
Only time would tell.

People always say, "Don't regret anything—it all teaches you something." And while I get that, there are a few things I'd do differently. And continuing to work through this time? That's one of them.

Eventually, we moved back to the hospital.

There was one major reason: the risk of a prolapsed cord. It was rare, but the doctors made it clear—it had to be managed instantly if it happened. With no membrane left, I was more at risk. And even though I kept telling myself, that won't happen to me, I knew deep down we couldn't take any more chances.

By now, we had made it to 27 weeks. One week away from the third trimester.

I was in good spirits. Feeling strong. That morning I'd had a lovely visit from my sister, Mum, my niece, and a girlfriend with her kids. There were baby cuddles, laughter I had to hold in, and nice chats that reminded me there was still joy in all of this.

Later that afternoon, I even stepped outside for some fresh air. It was a good day.

By 6 p.m., I was exhausted. I dozed off, feeling that familiar lower back ache from all the lying down. I'd also noticed more pressure in my belly, but during my last four-hourly check, the baby's heartbeat had been fine, so I stayed resting.

Then came the 9 p.m. check.

I was half asleep as the nurse scanned me. But I noticed something instantly. The heartbeat was slower. She reassured me—it was likely just a variation. But I knew better. I'd had enough checks by now to know when something was off.

I told Craig. He tried to comfort me. But there was this quiet urgency in my chest I couldn't shake. I remember hearing a message—somewhere between sleep and wakefulness:
Get up. You need to get up.

I ignored it at first. I didn't want to overreact. But after that check, I stood up to go to the bathroom. I wasn't even sure what I was looking for—just had a feeling. Maybe more fluid loss? Pressure?

And then—
I sat down...
looked down...
and everything stopped.

"Craig—the foot is hanging out!"

I screamed.
He hit the emergency alarms.

And just like that—everything changed.

CHAPTER 3

Will Jenkins

"Where There's a Will, There's a Way"

3.1 Welcome Will – The Miracle Baby

As I slowly opened my eyes to the bright lights and mechanical hum of the hospital, everything felt hazy. My body was heavy, still groggy from the anaesthetic, and my mind hadn't caught up to the fact that I had just given birth. Then I saw Craig standing beside me, beaming, holding a photo in his hand like it was the winning lottery ticket.

"Will's here. He made it," he said, his voice full of emotion.

I blinked. Wait, what?

Craig kept repeating it— "He made it, he made it"—like a mantra. I wanted to absorb those words, to feel the joy, but I was too disoriented. My mind and body were still trying to catch up with the whirlwind that had just happened.

Then I looked at the picture.

The image of our baby boy was both beautiful and utterly confronting. There were tubes snaking around his body, his tiny frame looking barely real—skin grey, wrinkled, and stretched too thin from oxygen loss. He didn't look like a newborn, or even like a human in that moment. He looked like something too fragile to exist in this world.

I just felt numb.

Moments later, they wheeled me into the NICU, still lying flat on the bed, to meet him for the first time. Through the foggy plastic of the humidity crib, I caught a glimpse of our son. Seven hundred grams. One pound, five ounces. So tiny he didn't look like he should be alive.

And then it hit me.

Tears poured down my cheeks—tears of joy, terror, awe, and something even deeper I couldn't name. I was a mum. This was my son.

Every part of me just wanted to scoop him up, hold him close, and whisper, It's okay, Mummy's here now. Like that would somehow make everything better. Like my touch alone could stabilise his tiny, fighting body. But I couldn't. He was too unstable. His life hung in the balance, and the next 24 hours would be critical. A nurse was monitoring him one-on-one.

What on earth had just happened?

You never know how you'll react in a situation like this until you're living it. And then—you just do. You survive. You override your own fear because there's no other choice. The body takes over. You get through it moment by moment.

It's only years later—if ever—that you find space to process what went down. And even then, it's messy. Fragmented. Painful. Most people don't go back there. Why would you, when pushing it aside feels easier?

Later that day, Craig and our obstetrician pieced the timeline together for me. The memory started trickling back. That strange bulge I had felt—what I thought might have been a foot—was actually the cord. I'd had a prolapsed cord, one of the most dangerous complications in pregnancy.

Within sixty seconds of Craig hitting the emergency button, the room was flooded with medical staff.

I remember being rushed toward the theatre, a nurse literally straddling me on the bed with her hand inside me, holding the cord in place, trying to stop it from cutting off Will's oxygen. I tried to breathe—tried not to spiral—but the thoughts came in waves.

I should've checked earlier. I should've got up. This is my fault. Why didn't I get up?

The nurse just held my gaze, calm but fierce, and kept telling me, "Breathe. It's not your fault. Just breathe."

Another nurse was inserting a cannula as we flew down the corridor. At the lift, we were met by the anaesthetist, and within seconds I was under. Gone. Just like that.

While I was unconscious, the registrar had to start the c-section. The on-call obstetrician arrived just in time to deliver Will, and by the time the placenta was delivered, our regular obstetrician had joined the team. The NICU staff were ready and waiting.

Will was born floppy. Lifeless. Not breathing.

He was given oxygen and nitric oxide.

And then—this part still gives me chills—one of the nurses later told me how, almost magically, he came to life in her hands. She described it like watching a flower unfold in the sun, slowly opening one petal at a time.

A delicate bloom in the middle of a crisis.

I asked her to retell that story again and again to visitors. I clung to it. That image brought me comfort. In the middle of trauma, it gave me something to hold onto—something magical that made me feel he was meant to be here.

Despite being squashed and twisted, despite concerns about his limbs, Will was a perfectly formed baby.

Except his lungs.

His lungs were underdeveloped and couldn't breathe on their own. Only time would tell how bad they really were.

I was eventually taken back up to my hospital room, where for the first time in what felt like days—but was probably just hours—I had a moment to myself.

The adrenaline was wearing off. The silence was deafening. And the fear? All-consuming.

I was terrified. Not just worried or anxious—terrified. I had no idea what was happening down in the NICU. Was Will okay? Was he even still alive? No one had updated me yet, and the not-knowing was a form of torture I wouldn't wish on anyone.

So, I did the only thing I could.

I prayed.

Over and over and over, I prayed. I didn't even know who I was praying to. God, the Universe, the angels, my grandma, spirit guides, white cockatoos—anyone. If you had a hotline to miracles, I was calling you.

I begged. Please let him be okay. Please let him stay.

And because I couldn't be in the room with him physically, I sent energy. Reiki-style. Healing-style. Desperate-mother-style. I tried to visualise his tiny body surrounded in light. I pictured every cell regenerating. I whispered, breathe, baby, breathe.

I sat there with tears streaming down my face, hands on my belly like maybe he could still feel me, and I focused on my breath. One inhale. One exhale. The only thing I could control.

Just breathe.

I never imagined I'd be the type to pray like that. But there I was, doing it with everything I had. And you know what? I believed it mattered. So, I didn't stop.

Later that night, a midwife I'd never met before—and would only see once again—walked in. She came quietly, but she brought with her something I didn't know I needed: perspective.

She said, "Your son was born tonight. No matter what happens, he will always be your son."

Something in me shifted.

Until that moment, I had been trying to protect myself—not fully allowing joy in. I was resisting the celebration, because what if it was ripped away? What if by morning, he wasn't here?

But she was right. He was born. And he was mine.

That was the moment I let myself feel it. I had a son. I was a mum. And even in the heartbreak and chaos, that was something to celebrate.

The next wave of energy hit me with a mission: Do something. Help him.

I couldn't breathe for him. I couldn't regulate his heart or build his lungs. But I could give him my milk.

So, I latched onto that like a lifeline. Expressing milk became my mission.

A midwife friend had once told me about double pumping to increase supply, and the memory came flying back like a divine download. Within minutes, I was barking instructions. I had Craig on one boob and the midwife on the other—yep, we were now a fully operational human dairy.

And I wasn't even producing milk yet. Just drops.

Tiny, sacred drops. One millilitre at a time.

But that 1ml felt like purpose. It felt like hope. Like maybe this was the thing I could do to keep my baby alive. And I clung to it with everything I had.

Will's first night was touch and go.

They threw everything they had at him—ventilation, meds, round-the-clock interventions—and still, his blood pressure was crashing, his oxygen levels refusing to stabilise.

Craig was called down to the NICU more than once that night. I can only imagine the fear he was feeling each time.

But somehow—somehow—our little boy made it through.

By morning, the doctors and nurses were amazed. Will had stabilised.

Not only that—he had stabilised so well that they were able to move him off the ventilator and onto CPAP, a supported breathing device. For a baby born so still and lifeless, this kind of turnaround wasn't just a good sign. It was a miracle.

We started to believe maybe—just maybe—we'd dodged a bullet.

This is how Will would live his entire life. He would be on the edge, literally on the brink of death, yet he kept coming back—surprising everyone, every time. He surprised everyone, again and again.

That's when we all started saying it—Where there's a Will, there's a way.

I believe that's what he came here to show us. That his name wasn't just a name—it was a truth. A promise. A message we would cling to more times than we could count.

And yeah, maybe we didn't name him "Will" for that reason at the time—but I don't believe in coincidences anymore.

This chapter—this part of our story—is by far the hardest to write.

How do you put your son's life into words?
How do you make it enough?
How do you honour something so sacred without breaking apart in the process?

Some days, I feel like I should split this whole thing into three chapters. Other days, I can't even face it—I skip ahead to lighter scenes, because this one is so heavy I can barely hold it.

The intensity of what happened in such a short space of time… it's still hard to comprehend.

And even now, part of me doesn't want to focus on the pain of his suffering. I want to share the good bits. The beauty. The love. The lessons. The joy.

But I know the darkness needs to be here too. Because without it, the light doesn't shine as brightly.

I know that sounds cliché—but when you've lived inside the walls of an intensive care unit, clichés become truths.

The NICU became our world.

The medical side of things—oxygen levels, blood gases, tube changes, stats—wasn't just background noise. It was our reality. It was the thing keeping him here.

And the staff? The doctors, the nurses, the midwives—they became our people. Our family. Our lifeline. This wasn't just their job. This was our home now.

As Will's mum, there's my story.
There's the story of those closest to us.
But most importantly, there's Will's.

And he never got to speak. He couldn't even breathe on his own.

So, I will speak for him. I will do my best to tell his story.

And I will keep going—even when it's hard.

Because he deserves that.

3.2 The Early Days

"Where there's a Will, there's a way."

That first week felt like I was being flung between heaven and hell on repeat. It was like being dragged between hope and heartbreak, again and again, without warning. I still can't fathom what it must have been like for him—our tiny 700-gram warrior.

One minute, we didn't know if he'd survive the emergency birth. The next, we were euphoric just to know he was alive. Then came the agonising wait—would he make it through the next 24 to 48 hours? When he did, and was moved off the ventilator to CPAP, we were back on a high.

Hope. Fear. Elation. Terror. Over and over again.

That first week felt like the longest of my life. And not being able to hold my baby made it even harder.

That need to hold your baby—it's not just emotional, it's primal. It lives deep inside you. You're meant to hold your baby. That's how it's supposed to be. Not being able to do that when they're suffering... it goes against everything in you. To be separated from your baby when they're suffering... it's incomprehensible.

You stand there, helpless, staring into an incubator for hours. If you're lucky, you're allowed to cup your hand gently around their tiny body. And in Will's case, he was so small my hand literally cupped around nearly his entire being.

But nothing in this journey unfolded how I imagined it 'should'.

The moment it really hit me was when I had to pack up and leave my hospital room—to move across the road to the apartment. I'd had plenty of teary moments during the pregnancy, but nothing prepared me for that.

As I walked into the apartment, it was like the last piece holding me together just snapped.

I collapsed onto the floor, sobbing. Scared. Helpless. Empty. Exhausted. Still in extraordinary physical pain from the caesarean. I was in shock that this was my life—that this was real.

The pain I felt for my son had taken over every part of me.

And when the tears finally stopped, I felt... nothing.

Completely shut down. Numb. I couldn't move, couldn't think, couldn't feel. It was like my entire system had short-circuited. The only way I could survive that moment was to retreat. I don't fully understand what happens in the body in times like that. It was as if my soul had briefly left the room.

In a strange way, I felt lifeless too.

But I knew I had to find something – I had to find some strength—because I had a son to fight for.

Nothing felt right.

How could this even be happening? It felt like I'd stepped into some kind of alternate universe. A parallel reality I never agreed to.

I started clinging to anything—pillows, teddy bears, anything to comfort me, anything that might fill the complete emptiness of not being able to hold my baby. I had to sleep cuddling something, even though sleep barely came.

Looking back on that time, I don't just feel my own pain—I feel it for every woman who's ever had to leave a hospital without her child. For every mum who's lost a baby. For every parent who's had to sit beside a suffering child, completely helpless.

This is the silent heartbreak and pain millions of women carry across the world. And it's brutal.

Life just isn't fair sometimes. It's not always how it's meant to be.

3.3 We're Gonna Love You Like We're Gonna Lose You

And boy, did we need to cling to every ounce of hope we had.

After the initial honeymoon period—the first couple of weeks when it felt like we might've dodged the bullet—came the first real crash.

Craig and I were back at the apartment taking a short break when the phone rang. Will had been put back on the ventilator. He was struggling on CPAP, and the doctor on shift had made the call to reintubate him so his lungs could rest and, hopefully, grow stronger.

Medically, it was the right decision. But emotionally—it was a devastating blow.

The call came from a doctor who was covering for Will's usual team. He was blunt, clinical, and cold. No warmth. No softness. No attempt to meet us as two terrified parents on the other end of the line.

This wasn't the first time I'd felt his detachment. He was one of those old-school types—"doctor knows best," brusque, unapproachable, and completely shut off from questions. He didn't make space for conversation, let alone compassion. Just, I'll tell you what's happening, when it's happening—don't ask questions.

It was the opposite of Will's regular doctor, who treated us with such dignity and care. That contrast made it even harder. Most of the staff at the hospital were incredible—truly exceptional—and I want to be clear about that. But this one experience stayed with me.

Because he wasn't just speaking to a patient. He was speaking to the mother of a child barely clinging to life.

Sometimes I wonder—do people like that just get numb to death? Did he have empathy to begin with? Every time I asked a question or pushed for more information, I felt his resistance. His irritation. Like my concern was a nuisance.

And even though I understood that detachment might be a form of protection, I couldn't accept it. Because when you're in that position—when you hold power over a child's life—empathy shouldn't be optional.

About a month after Will passed away, I saw that same doctor at my local coffee shop. He was sitting there with two young children, quietly sipping a coffee.

The rage rose up inside me so intensely.

I wanted to walk straight over and ask him, how would you feel if one of your children were dying—and the doctor in charge spoke to you like you didn't matter? If I'm honest I felt like I wanted to physically punch him. I've never ever felt that before. I didn't, of course. I walked away.

Later I even wrote a letter of complaint, but I never sent it. Not because my feelings weren't real, but because I had more important things to carry: my grief, my love, my son's legacy. And because all of the other doctors had been beyond exceptional.

In the end, I chose to lay that battle down.

Today, with distance, I can see that maybe he was carrying his own unspoken battles. Perhaps numbness was the only way he knew to keep going. And maybe, if I'm honest, it wasn't even his job to comfort me. His job — like every doctor and nurse in that hospital — was to make life and death decisions under impossible pressure.

And the truth is, nothing he said could have taken away the pain I was in. That doesn't erase how it felt at the time, but it helps me hold it now with more compassion — not just for him, but for all the doctors and nurses who face the weight of these jobs, every single day.

—

Will going back on the ventilator marked the start of a tumultuous few weeks—some of the most terrifying of our lives.

We came close to losing him.
More than once.

Life on a ventilator is incredibly uncomfortable. Will was more restricted in his movements, and every time the tube dislodged—which happened several times—it triggered a Code Red.

It was every parent's worst nightmare.

When that alarm went off, everything became a race against time: Could the nurses keep him going long enough on the resuscitation machine until a doctor arrived to reintubate him? Would his lungs collapse? Could he be brought back? There was no certainty. Only waiting. Only fear.

One night stands out above the rest.

Craig and I walked into the NICU to the sound of alarms blaring and a swarm of doctors and nurses around Will. They had already reintubated him, but he wasn't picking up.

He just lay there. Frozen.

I remember the room felt suspended in time.

Everyone looked like they were moving in slow motion—even though, in reality, I know they were doing everything they could. But in that moment, it felt like no one was doing enough.

I pushed my way to his crib, grabbed his tiny hand, and locked eyes with him.

"You're not leaving me," I said, voice breaking, my whole body shaking. "Will you are not leaving me. You Hold on. Please. Please bubba. You're not leaving us. You're going to be okay. I'm right here. Keep fighting. Mum's got you."

I didn't let go.

Somehow—whether it was the medicine, the touch, the timing, or sheer Will—he stabilised. He picked up.

We didn't leave his side that night. Craig and I tag-teamed through the early hours, taking turns in the small family room beside the unit. The kind of room no one ever wants to need.

When I look back on that night, two things really hit me.

The first: Should I have let him go?
Was that the moment he was ready to leave—and I kept pulling him back through more pain and suffering?

I'll never know. But what I do know, with absolute certainty, is that I wasn't ready to say goodbye. Not even close.

The second: how differently Craig and I handled moments like these.

I went straight into it—asking questions, pushing for answers, doing everything I could to change the outcome. Craig stayed back. He was concerned, of course, but he didn't engage in the same way.

He saw things. He had questions too. But he didn't speak them.

In fact, there were times when my questioning frustrated him. He didn't understand my need to fight so fiercely for information, to be in it. Our different approaches clashed during Will's care—again and again.

There were a few times he did speak up, usually after I'd insisted. I'm sure he'd have his own version of that. But from where I stood, I often felt like I was fighting alone.

Those differences didn't disappear. If anything, they got louder during our grief. The ways we each tried to survive just kept pulling us further apart.

There were more courses of steroids. More blood transfusions. And then, the conversation we'd been dreading.

We were sat down by Will's doctor—and the head of the unit—and told some harsh, unavoidable realities.

Will wasn't going to make it.
It wasn't if. It was when.

They needed us to understand that.

And to their credit, they delivered the news gently. They were caring and genuine. But how are you supposed to accept something like that?

How do you sit there and listen to someone tell you your son is going to die—and just… take it in?

I couldn't.

Because the moment I accepted it, I'd have to stop fighting.
And I wasn't ready to stop.

I started researching anything and everything—stem cells in the US, a trial in Korea, lung transplants, devices being used in the States. Anything.

But none of it could help Will.
He was simply too small. Too fragile.

Still—we kept going. Because what else do you do when it's your child?

During this time, Will was also placed on morphine to help with the pain caused by the ventilator. The machine had damaged his vocal cords, so we rarely heard a whimper from him—let alone a proper cry.

It breaks me to think he might've been crying, screaming for help… and I just didn't hear him.

One day, Will was especially unsettled—tossing and turning, clearly distressed. Nothing we tried helped. He wasn't himself.

A nurse trained in pain management called a meeting with the head nurse and the doctor. She questioned how much pain Will was in… and whether it was acceptable.

And just like that, I went from being the mum who fought for everything… to feeling like I was being judged.

I felt sick.

Sick thinking he might've been in more pain than I realised.
Sick thinking that I was the one driving the decisions that caused it.
Sick feeling like I was failing at the one job I had—to protect him.

It was the first time I felt like I wasn't fully supported—like people were questioning whether I was doing the right thing.

But I understood it, too.

They were advocating for him. That's their job. And ultimately, it's mine too. As Will's mum, I was trying to do everything I could to give him a chance. I thought I was doing right by him.

But where is that line?
The line between pushing for life and pushing through pain?

At that point, I was still ready to fight.
And so I did.

We adjusted his care, and Will did settle. He looked more comfortable. The team agreed.

And for that moment, at least—I breathed a little easier.

Another major shift happened during Will's ventilator days—and it wasn't medical.

It was Craig.

One day, out of nowhere, he looked me in the eye and said with total certainty, "Will's going to survive."

He wasn't just hoping. He knew. He held Will's hand, stared into his little face, and told him it was going to be okay.

And in that moment, a new energy entered the room. A lift. His belief gave me belief. For a while, I rode that wave with him.

But looking back, I think that moment marked something else.

A turning point.

A part of Craig shut down—like a switch flipped. I think it's what he needed to do to cope. To take control of the chaos. To function.

But it was also a part of him I haven't seen since.

Before that, I had never seen Craig cry so much. We shared some of our most vulnerable moments in those weeks—crying in each other's arms, holding each other up, sometimes literally picking one another up off the floor.

I look back on those moments as so intimate. I think he might see them as weakness.

After that shift, Craig's tears stopped. I mean completely stopped.

Whenever I got upset, he'd just say, "It'll be okay."
Whenever I needed to talk about the possibility of losing Will, he'd shut it down.

One day, when I was struggling, he even suggested I go home if I couldn't handle it.

That was our first real fight during Will's care. I was stunned. How dare he?

He was still supportive in some ways, but something had changed. He was shorter with me. Less available. Less... there.

And the hardest part?
We never fully got that closeness back.

Not even when Liv was born.

It breaks my heart to say it. We had been at our closest in the most fragile, intimate moments—and then it was gone forever.

I realised a lot later that the version of who I thought my husband was to me was dying too.

I don't know why. Maybe it wasn't a place Craig wanted to be again. I can't speak for him.

But I know this:
Since Will, I've become more honest. More open. More vulnerable. I ask for help now. I speak my truth.

And that's one of Will's gifts to me.

Meanwhile, Will was still fighting on the ventilator, but it wasn't looking good. We were told to bring the family in to say goodbye.

This time, it really was a matter of days.

My only way of coping was to hold him. To feel his body against mine.

So, I did.

I took him out for a cuddle and sat in the recliner chair beside his cot, placing him gently on my chest, right over my heart. I tucked him into my jumper and held him as close as I possibly could.

I didn't want to let go.

I couldn't.

What if this really was the last time? If he only had a few days left, I was going to hold him for every second I could.

I stayed there for eight hours straight.

Eventually, my bladder and my exploding boobs won—I had to go to the toilet and express. But I only moved because I had no choice.

Those eight hours were everything.

They were full of tears. Full of fear. But also full of something else—something deeper. It felt kind of spiritual.

Connection.

Presence.

A love so pure and so deep I felt like time disappeared.

Looking back, I know I touched something truly sacred in those hours. I felt what it means to love someone with your whole being.

I'll never forget that time.

Those eight hours are etched into my body. My memory. My heart.

And I will always cherish them.

3.4 The Will to Fight

Maybe it was just a coincidence.

Maybe it was timing.

But after that hug... Will picked up.

Part of me wants to say it was a miracle. A quiet healing. A reminder of the power of love.

And that's comforting—until I start thinking:
If love is that powerful..., why isn't he still here?

That's when the questions come in like a wave.
Was I not loving him hard enough?
Was I not evolved enough to hold space for him in this world?
Was Craig and my relationship not strong enough as a family unit for Will to stay?

Why couldn't he make it in the world?

The only answer that brings me peace is this:
Will and I had a bond so strong—so deep—that he had to come meet me in the physical world.

I mean... how else do you survive your waters breaking at 15 weeks?

So that's the truth I hold onto. Not just as a passing thought—but as something I have to believe.
It's the only way forward.

And so, when Will picked up after that hug—what felt like a genuine miracle—we shifted from preparing to say goodbye... to planning his next step forward.

The decision was made to try removing him from the ventilator and place him on a breathing device called NIPPV. It was a stronger version of CPAP—he would still need significant assistance, but it meant he'd be breathing with support, not because of a machine.

To give him the best shot, the plan was to start another round of steroids and attempt the transition once they had reached their peak effect. That window—those few days—was crucial.

We knew: if this worked, it was a step toward life.
If it didn't... it might be the beginning of the end.

The doctors and nurses remained professional, careful with their words, but I could feel it in the room: no one was holding high hopes.

And to be fair—there wasn't much reason to.

His X-rays showed some of the worst chronic lung disease they'd seen in a living baby. His oxygen saturation was chronically low. His carbon dioxide was elevated.

But still... I just knew.

I knew he'd make it through this step.
And he did.

We were celebrating.

Will had made it off the ventilator and onto NIPPV. It felt like a huge leap — a step away from death and a step toward home.

There were so many benefits to this change, but the biggest one — well, for me anyway — was that I could finally do some proper mum things.

Not much, but enough.

Under careful supervision, I was allowed to pick my baby up from his cot and place him back down. I got to tuck him in.

I got to be a mum.

We had this beautiful lullaby CD we'd play for Will every night. I haven't been able to listen to it since. I tried once, long after he passed, thinking I might play it for Liv. But the moment it started, it was too much — like being time-warped straight back.

Music does that. It holds memories.
Maybe one day I'll press play again and let the beautiful memories in, not just the pain.

One of the most magical moments in that "NIPPV window" was giving Will his very first bath — not a sponge bath, but a proper warm-water bath.

I was so nervous, trying to juggle the cords and equipment, but as soon as he touched the water, he just melted into my arms.

His whole body let go. I didn't even realise how tense he had been until I felt him relax.

He loved it. And I did too.

It really is the simple joys.

I still cherish bath and shower time with Liv — it's often our reconnect time after long or challenging days. Until writing this, I hadn't really made the connection… maybe that bonding time came from Will. Another gift.

We even got to dress him — briefly.

Will ran hot because of his elevated CO_2 levels, so clothes didn't last long. He was my little nudist son… and I was totally cool with that.

But there was one day we dressed him in a Wallabies jumpsuit I'd bought when I first found out I was pregnant.

That photo sits beside my bed.

He looked so proud, so strong. And I remember thinking — how cool is it that he wore a Wallabies jersey before he even reached his due date?

He may never have run onto a field, never played a sport — but in that moment, he wore his strength. And let's be honest, the Wallabies could've used some of his fight.

When I first got pregnant, I remember wondering what sport he'd play, what team he'd be on, whether he'd be any good at it. And I hoped, even then, that he'd be okay with himself if he wasn't.

Funny how perspective changes.

Now all I wanted was for my son to survive. In any form.

One of the highlights of this phase was Will's regular physio sessions.

They felt proactive — like we were doing something not just to survive, but to build toward a future.

Chest-opening movements, limb stretches to keep his body flexible from all the time spent in bed, even developmental assessments like any other baby might get.

He loved them.

And so did we.

There were so many moments in NICU where we felt helpless. These weren't those. These were the moments where we felt… hopeful.

But my favourite moment — maybe of the entire NICU journey — was the day one of the nurses suggested we try Will in what's called a Fraser chair.

It's basically a supported little seat with straps that sits in the cot and allows the baby to sit upright.

We sat Will up in that chair and I swear to God, the look on his face was priceless.

He looked around the room — his home — and saw the world from a whole new perspective.

No more staring at a white ceiling. No more only seeing things from flat on his back.

He was upright. He was alert. He was alive.

I couldn't stop smiling. I'm not even sure why that moment brought so much joy, but I think I felt his excitement.

It was so simple. Just sitting him in a chair—who would've thought it could bring that much joy?

For about a week, maybe a little more, things felt... lighter.

We had entered what I called our "purple patch."
The pressures of ICU life weren't gone — but they had softened.

I got to focus more on the day-to-day mum stuff.
Feeds, physio, cuddles.

But, like all waves in NICU, the calm didn't last.

Will's oxygen saturations started dropping again.

He was placed back on 1:1 care. His monitors would sound constantly — too low again.

Little tweaks to his position, to his device, to the bed settings were being made around the clock.

Even feeding him became a careful process.

Too full a belly, and it would press against his lungs. Digesting required energy — and Will didn't have much to spare.

All of this was just to keep him breathing.

Just to keep him alive.

I had countless meetings with the dietitian, trying to adjust the feeding schedule. He needed calories to grow. He needed to grow to build new lung tissue. That was his only path to long-term survival.

But too much food, and it could push him too far the other way.

It was a razor-thin margin.

And I'm sure at times I was demanding. Probably exhausting. But this was my son. Guidelines are guidelines — but Will wasn't a number. He was a human.

That became the heart of so many discussions — with his doctor, nurses, the nurse manager, the head doctors, the social worker, the respiratory team from Lady Cilento.

No one had seen a case like his.
His numbers didn't make sense. His X-rays didn't line up with his outcomes.

And yet... he kept living.

That's one of the things I loved most about his doctor and the team. Despite the data, they always returned to this:

"We are treating the baby in front of us. Not the numbers. Not the textbook. Will."

That approach is something I carry with me still.
As a mother to Liv.
As a woman.
As a wellbeing practitioner.

We meet people where they are.
We honour who is in front of us — not just what they present on paper.

I remember being so focused on the milestone — that Will had made it off the ventilator — that I didn't fully grasp what he was going through.

Not at the time.

It's only now, years later, that I can begin to comprehend just how hard he was working… just to be here.

Every single breath was a battle.

You know that burning feeling when you go for a long run and you're gasping to catch your breath?
That was Will.
Every. Single. Breath.

He lived that way.

He fought that way.

And honestly, it still breaks my heart when I sit with that reality.

Recently, while I was writing and reliving these moments, a friend of mine was doing a challenge to raise awareness for cystic fibrosis.

He invited people to breathe through a straw — just a regular drinking straw — to experience what it's like.

So, I tried it.

And within seconds, I was gasping. Panicking. Tears welling.

It hit me hard.

That was how my baby lived. And I... I kept pushing him to keep going.

How did I not stop to fully understand that at the time?

I just hope with every piece of my heart that Will's life wasn't only pain.
That he had moments — even tiny ones — of joy, of lightness.
That he felt our love.
That there were pain-free moments I didn't see, but he felt.

I'll never know for sure.
And that unknowing — it's its own kind of grief.

And here's the truth I don't often say out loud:

Sometimes I get angry.

Angry that people walk around breathing effortlessly and wasting it.
People who live without really living.
People who complain about the smallest things while my son fought like hell just to take a single breath.

That contrast—between Will's courage and others' complacency—cuts deep.

And here's the harder truth:
A lot of that anger... is actually at myself.

Even since Will passed, I've caught myself coasting through days, not fully appreciating this gift of life the way I said I would.

Not breathing it in, not showing up fully, not being the version of me he saw.

And maybe—just maybe—those people who frustrate me are reflecting back the parts of me I'm still learning to love.

I need to BE more.
I must be more.

But I'll come back to that later.

—

It wasn't long before the Will in front of us began to struggle. He was running out of breath, out of fight—and then came the big crash. Everything started to slow: his breathing, his heart rate. His colour turned grey. As we held him, he seemed to be becoming more lifeless by the minute.

I think I was too.

I couldn't comprehend what was happening. All I wanted to do was hold him. I don't remember much of what happened that afternoon and night. The family came up to say goodbye. I remember a very emotional farewell between my sister Lyndsay and Will—his aunty. They had such a special connection. Then we were moved out of the NICU into a private hospital room to have some space while he died.

Amongst it all, Will was given one final steroid dose in a desperate attempt to keep him going. But it didn't seem to be doing anything.

That whole night is such a blur. Will, Craig and I all lay together in a single bed—for what we thought would be our final night as a family. A nurse stayed in the room the entire time, continuing his medication and feeding schedule. Some of Will's most-loved nurses came in to see him, but I barely remember any of it. I was done. Exhausted on every level. Numb. I just lay there holding Will for whatever time we had left.

Throughout the night, his levels dropped so low that it seemed any breath could be his last.

But as dawn broke and we slowly woke from whatever sleep we got, Will was still with us. Not only that—his colour was returning. His oxygen levels were back in range. For a moment, I honestly wondered if I had dreamt the whole thing. But no—the steroids had kicked in. Somehow, they had worked.

The next thing I remember, we were taking Will out of the room in a pram, onto the grass. In palliative care, you're allowed to do that.

We sat in the sun as a family. Will got to feel the warmth on his face, the wind in his hair, the grass beneath him. He heard the birds. I was so grateful, so happy that he got to experience that. That we got to experience that with him.

We spent about a week or so in the private room on palliative care, where we got to enjoy our daily outings to the grassed area. Just laying there, being — the three of us together. The Bob Marley song Three Little Birds, with the line "Don't worry, be happy, every little thing gonna be alright" came on in the car several times on out trips to the hospital, and Craig saw us as the three little birds. I thought it was a sign. I guess it was, in a roundabout kind of way.

Some of my favourite photos and memories were made out on that grass. One of the most special was when my sister and niece visited, and the two cousins — born so close in time — got to sit side by side. My sister and I had been pregnant together with our first babies, excited that they would grow up side by side. That never happened… but we got that moment.

That week gave us, for the first time, a sense of privacy as a family. The nurses only came in at set times. The rest of the time, it was just us — the three little birds.

One morning, I sat in the reclining chair holding Will while Craig made me a cup of coffee. I flicked on the TV. It might sound like nothing, but I remember it so clearly — because it felt, for a brief moment, like we were living a normal family life. I was so, so grateful for those simple things. That morning gave me such huge perspective… the kind I've lost at times since but keep trying to find again — for Will.

Because even in that glimpse of sunshine … the hard conversations were waiting just around the corner.

—

Firstly, the respiratory team came over from the children's hospital Lady Cilento to talk about Will's future. As he was now approaching term, he'd soon age out of the neonatal unit and would need to be transferred to the children's ward. I remember the respiratory physician — a kind man — explaining that he had never seen a baby like Will survive. He was trying to gently prepare me for what was coming, to make sure I understood just how serious things were.

But I still hadn't fully grasped what palliative care meant. Not really.

I remember interrupting him and saying, "You're not God. So how can you tell me for sure who lives and who dies?"

Because I still believed. I needed to believe. I was clinging to the idea of a miracle — and I believed, deep down, that Will might be one.

We had a video meeting with the Sunshine Coast Hospital to discuss transferring Will so we could be closer to home. We'd been away for more than four months — I hadn't been home once. But the logistics didn't stack up. The equipment wasn't suitable, the setup didn't feel right, and the idea of taking Will away from the team who had cared for him so lovingly felt too risky.

What sealed the decision for me was a single line: "If he's in palliative care, he won't be given antibiotics — only medication to keep him comfortable."

After everything we'd been through, the thought of not treating a simple infection was something I just couldn't accept. Not then.

There were other conversations too — about the possibility of a tracheostomy ventilator. It would mean Will being hooked up to a breathing machine for life, through a surgical incision in his neck. Brutal stuff. Not the life I'd dreamed of for my boy. But I still looked into it. It needed government approval, so I started reaching out to people, trying to find a way. But the truth was, Will wasn't strong enough. Even if we got the green light, the procedure could kill him — and even then, it wouldn't change the outcome. The damage to his lungs was too great.

We were also offered the option of taking Will home for his final days. That one was tough. Because for so long, all I'd wanted was to bring my baby boy home — to finally have our family under one roof.

I spoke to a friend who had lost her first child. She gently asked me to consider whether I'd be able to live in that space afterwards, knowing Will had died there. Because some memories never leave you.

There were other questions too — how would we manage the practicalities? What if something went wrong? What if he didn't pass peacefully? There were just too many unknowns.

The palliative care team walked us through every option, step by step. They were calm, kind, and detailed. And yet... even as I nodded and asked questions, a part of me still didn't believe we were in palliative care.

Because Will looked like he was doing so well.

—

Our time in the private room was up. We'd already stayed longer than most families get, and we had to decide what came next. After a lot of discussion, Craig and I chose to go back into the NICU—back to the pod—where Will would be under full medical care again. It meant he'd be treated with everything available: medications, injections, round-the-clock management.

We made the decision based on what we saw in front of us. Will wasn't getting weaker—he was gaining strength. How do you accept palliative care when your baby is showing signs of fight? When he's defied the odds again and again? When you genuinely believe he might be your miracle?

But not everyone agreed with our decision. One nurse—one of our favourites, actually—asked me gently, "Who are you doing this for?" I know it came from love and from her wanting what was best for Will. That's her job. And even though she never said anything like that again—and was incredibly supportive afterwards—I've never forgotten those words. I've carried them with me ever since. I've done a lot of soul searching around that question.

Walking back into the pod was one of the hardest things I've ever done. I felt the shift in energy. Maybe it was just my own guilt or my own perception, but I sensed that some of the nurses looked at us differently after that. It was a raw, emotionally exhausting few days.

One thing I've come to understand is that unless you've ever had to make a decision like that—about the life of your child—you simply can't know what it feels like. I couldn't have known either, not until I was standing in those shoes. And honestly, I had judged others in the past. Not harshly, but I definitely held opinions without knowing the full story. That experience changed me. It has made me more compassionate. Less certain. Less quick to assume.

And one thing I want to say clearly is this: everyone, apart from Craig and I, knew Will wasn't going to make it. And still, they showed up. They gave their time, their care, their presence. All while carrying their own lives and burdens. For that, I am deeply, deeply grateful.

In the end, I just kept coming back to this: how do you know when enough is enough? When do you stop fighting for your child? What is a life worth? Who decides what is best? And how do you make peace with that decision?

People had told me earlier, "When the time comes, you'll know." And I didn't feel it then. Whether that was Will holding on for me or me not ready to let go—I'll never know. But I knew in my heart it wasn't time yet. That time would come. But not then.

—

When we moved back to the pod, we were able to keep doing some of the palliative care activities we'd started—like taking Will outside. We even bought a baby swing and got to place him in it beside his cot. Looking back, I realise how lucky we were to be able to do these things in an intensive care unit. I'll always be grateful for that. Those moments in the swing, the sunshine, the air, are some of the most beautiful of my life. They are proof that Will had joy in his life too.

I also wanted to celebrate him—so on his original due date, a group of my close girlfriends came up and we had brunch across the road from the hospital. It felt really special to celebrate Will that day. I was in the mindset of marking every milestone. It was a little pocket of normality, and being surrounded by girlfriends filled my soul. That moment gave me the energy I needed to keep going, even though I had no idea just how hard the next couple of weeks would be.

Then, Will reached 100 days.

The hospital made a cake—"Happy 100 Days, Will Daley." (Yes, Daley. Because after three years of marriage, I still hadn't changed my Medicare card, another frustration for Craig which I did get.)

We sat there, Craig and I, with Will in my arms, while the wonderful nurses and Will's doctor sang happy birthday. It was one of the few moments I let myself feel truly happy. We even had happy tears. It was a beautiful family moment—another little high in a sea of lows. Never in my wildest dreams did I think Will had only four days left.

But after that celebration, Will began to deteriorate again.

And this time, we knew—we were truly out of options.

Not just running low. Actually out.

We had given every treatment possible. We'd gone outside the box with experimental treatment. We'd already done the palliative care round and come back. There was no plan left. No "next step." Nothing to pivot to. The only thing that could save Will now was a miracle—the kind that brings death to life, the kind that delivers new lungs from heaven itself.

And, for some reason, I still thought that miracle might come.

Until I saw Will on Day 103.

3.5 Goodbye Will

That night, around 2 a.m., I got a phone call from one of the nurses. They couldn't stabilise Will—he was very unsettled. Craig and I rushed straight to the hospital. As soon as I walked in and saw the look on the nurse's face, I knew something was wrong. There was a quiet urgency in the room, and the nurses moved around us with a level of care and empathy that said more than words ever could.

Something was different that night. Will looked at me differently. As I stood by his cot with my hand resting gently on him, I felt something shift—something you can't quite explain. I've since learned this is what people mean when they talk about an inner knowing. A quiet, awareness that the time is near.

Strangely, while I was emotional on the outside, a deep calm rose within me. Not peace exactly, maybe more like a guided stillness—something that felt like it was taking care of me, holding me, walking me through it. That's when I began to speak to Will.

I told him how much I loved him, how proud I was to be his mum, how much joy he had brought into my life. I thanked him for his unbelievable fight to stay in this physical world with us. I apologised for any pain I had caused him, letting him know that it came from my desperate need to give him life.

I told him he would always be my son. And with tears in my eyes, I gave him permission to go.

I told Will that I understood if he needed to return to his angelic work—that if his spirit needed to leave, we would be okay. Mum and Dad would be okay. And he would always be with us.

It was something I didn't mention to Craig at the time. He was busy adjusting the snorkel, trying to improve Will's oxygen saturation, speaking with the nurses about what else might help. But I knew. Deep down, I knew it was different this time.

While Will was sleeping, we returned to the apartment to quickly shower and refuel before heading back in. When we arrived, one of Will's favourite nurses—someone who had watched over him so closely during his time there—looked at me with knowing eyes and said quietly, "He's not okay."

"I know," I replied.

She explained that the way Will was moving his head—arching, struggling—was a sign he was fighting for air. His oxygen levels were so low, and his body was reacting the way someone does when they're drowning. I asked her if she thought it was time. She didn't need to answer. I knew.

I begged—what could we do to keep him out of pain? To make this as peaceful as possible? He had already been given morphine, and they assured us he would continue receiving it to stay comfortable. She suggested removing the snorkel—the one he had hated from the day he was born, always trying to push it away—and instead placing him on a light oxygen flow through two tiny nasal tubes.

That way, he could breathe more freely... and we could take him outside and him be free. Free in nature away from all the machines and wires and masks that had confined him since birth.

This was the moment. Once we made that change, there would be no going back. We were gently guided through the process, told that we could take all the time we needed. First, we would go outside to spend our final day together. Then, when we were ready, we would move to a private room to say goodbye.

It was the decision I had been fighting for six months—ever since my waters broke. And yet, I was surprisingly calm. Or maybe not calm... more like numb. As if I were moving through another altered reality where time slowed, and nothing felt quite real.

But my inner knowing was strong. I knew this was the moment it was meant to happen. I had spoken with Will. That conversation had set him free. He had fought so hard to stay—for me, for us. And I had held on with every ounce of strength I had, until finally, I was ready to face the truth.

Or... had I given up?

Had I lost faith in a miracle?

Was I not strong enough to keep believing?

Those questions will never have answers. So, I've had to choose how I live with them. And I choose to believe in love. In the sacredness of our bond. In the strength of our connection that goes beyond this life.

But there's one part of that conversation that still haunts me. I spoke for Craig. I told Will his dad would be okay.

What right did I have to say that?

The truth is... I don't think Craig was ready. His journey has been his own—complex and painful in ways I'll never fully understand.

I said to Will that his dad would be okay. But I don't know if that's true. I can't speak for Craig. And maybe that's where I went wrong.

I made a promise I had no power to keep.

In the years that followed, I often carried a quiet guilt—wondering if I had broken my word to Will. Not out of neglect or betrayal, but because I simply couldn't control how things unfolded.

All I can do now is hope that, in time, Craig finds his own healing... and that Will understands.

So just like that, Will was removed from his mask, placed gently in a pram, and we stepped outside together as a family—nurse and oxygen tank in tow.

What would you choose to do on your final day on Earth?

It's something I've spent a lot of time reflecting on—those last moments with Will. I often wonder if we gave him what he would've wanted. I hope so.

The most important part was that we were all together. Somehow, in the middle of so much heartbreak, we were just able to be. We sat and lay down together on the grass, still within the hospital grounds, the fresh air brushing against us. We held Will close, gave him gentle cuddles, held his tiny hand, looked into his eyes without the barrier of a mask. We stroked his hair and arms, covered him in kisses. We were just there—being love and giving love.

Will's skin was pale from the lack of oxygen. His eyes dark, tired, with little bags beneath them. His breathing had slowed and become irregular. Watching someone breathe like that—knowing they're approaching the end of their life—is surreal. And yet, I've never been more present in my life.

I wasn't thinking about tomorrow. There was no tomorrow. Just now. And I didn't want to be anywhere else.

That moment is imprinted in me. I can take myself back to it anytime. It plays like a 3D movie in my mind—every sight, sound, and sensation vivid and alive in my body. Sometimes when I close my eyes, it feels like Will is still right there in my arms. Maybe, in some way, he still is.

Then something beautiful happened. In a synchronistic moment, my mum called to say she was on her way. She never did that. Visits were always planned and scheduled. But somehow, she knew. She had to be there. And she arrived just in time for a few last cuddles with Will. It felt like a small miracle—not only for him, but for mum and me too.

In the background, I noticed some of the doctors and nurses pause by the window. Others walked quietly past, stealing one last look at Will. They gave us space— for our final moments together.

As the afternoon wore on and the sun shifted away from the grass where we sat, we made the decision to move inside to a private room. Will's doctor returned to check on him and made sure he wasn't in pain. He was given a little more morphine.

Despite the reputation of hospital rooms being cold and sterile, this one felt different. It was warm—maybe not in temperature, but in energy. Maybe it was all the love in that room. We had the music channel playing softly on the TV— nothing specific I can remember, just a gentle, relaxing background that seemed to comfort us all.

The nurse suggested we give Will a bath.

Craig—the doer—took charge. He bathed Will gently, while I stayed close, holding Will's hand, gazing into his eyes, soaking up every final detail. His eyes looked glassy from the morphine. I wasn't sure if he was still fully with us, or if part of him had already started to leave.

After the bath, we dried him carefully and moved to the bench seat by the window. I cradled him in my arms, and the nurse quietly explained what would come next. When we were ready, she said, she would remove the oxygen. He would pass peacefully.

Fear rushed in.

I wasn't ready.

All I wanted to know was whether it would hurt him. The nurse reassured me—because of the morphine, he wouldn't be in pain. She gently warned us that sometimes the body makes strange noises as it dies. But even with her reassurance, I was scared. Deeply scared.

I needed more time. And so, I held him longer.

Craig was tucked in right beside us. I kept stroking Will's curly ginger hair, tracing his chubby cheeks with my fingertips, whispering how much I loved him. Telling him he was the best thing that had ever happened to me. That I would love him forever.

It's hard to explain what you feel in that moment. I wasn't howling. I wasn't screaming. The pain was too deep for that. It turned to stillness, to numbness. I knew it was happening but couldn't fathom how it could be happening.

Will's breathing became slower, longer, more irregular. He drifted between unconsciousness and tiny, tender moments of awareness. Every so often he'd open an eye, just the slightest, as if to let me know he was still listening.

A part of me still held hope.

Maybe, when the oxygen was removed, he'd keep breathing. Maybe a miracle would come.

But then... it was time.

I was still nursing Will in my arms, Craig right beside me. As the nurse leaned in to remove the oxygen, I reached out with my free hand and squeezed Craig's tightly.

And then, something happened I will never forget.

In that exact moment, Will opened his eyes. His little body almost sat up as he took one deep, final gasp—his eyes locking with mine, then shifting to Craig's.

Then he gently closed them again and relaxed, peacefully, back into my arms.

There he was. No mask. No tubes. Just Will—resting in my arms like a baby should.

The only time I got to see and hold my son completely free like that... was after he had already left.

But he didn't pass immediately. His heart kept beating. The nurse continued checking, waiting for that final moment. He held on. He was so strong.

And then, at 5:45 p.m., Will was pronounced dead.

I was holding a lifeless body.

My son. My greatest love. The little boy I had imagined spending a lifetime with... gone after 104 days.

I didn't want to move.
And I don't just mean physically—I didn't want to move on. Because how do you leave... without your son?

The next step was letting Will go so he could spend time in his dad's arms.

Craig had so lovingly let me hold Will through his last moments and he needed his time. He walked slowly around the room holding Will, talking softly to his son. Then suddenly, the emotions bubbled up and overflowed. Craig—who could suppress anything, who rarely cried—burst into tears.

Will looked so much like him. Craig kept lifting him up beside his face, as if trying to memorise every detail. Watching them together broke me even more.

In that moment, the life I had envisioned for them—their future, their bond, all the milestones and memories—I saw it flash before my eyes. And then fade, as I realised it was never to be.

Then Will was passed back to me.

But now... now he was starting to feel cold. His colouring had changed—that unmistakable shift when the body lets go. And yet, in my eyes, he still felt so alive. I held him close, resting his head on my chest, willing the warmth of that moment to stay in my body forever.

Then something happened that I still can't fully explain.

I began to feel heat.

A rush of warmth, like blood pumping fast beneath his skin—but he was already gone. I felt it pulse near my heart, exactly where Will's head was resting. A surge of energy. Strong. Undeniable. It lasted maybe ten, fifteen seconds. I even screamed out to the nurse as it was so intense, wondering—just for a moment—was he coming back to life?

But then it stopped.

I turned to Craig and said, "I think... I think something moved from him into me." That's how it felt. Like Will's spirit had entered my heart.

I sat in that feeling for a while, just holding him, breathing it in. Then Will went back to Craig for more final cuddles... before returning to me again.

But when Craig handed him back that second time, something had changed.

This time, it was like holding a rag doll. The energy—the lifeforce—was gone. I looked at him and softly said, "This isn't Will."

Part of me felt cold saying it. Like I was being heartless. But I wasn't. I was speaking a deeper truth. A knowing beyond logic.

Only recently, I read a line that helped it all make sense: "Beyond the rational isn't irrational—it's non-rational."

Just because there wasn't a logical explanation didn't mean I was losing my mind.

I've spoken to spiritual mentors and healers about that moment. And I know—I know—what I felt wasn't imagined. It was Will's spirit leaving his body and entering mine.

He's with me. Always has been, ever since. I carry his spirit in my heart.

That was the gift he left me with.

And with that inner knowing, I held him one final time... before placing him gently into the arms of one of his favourite nurses. She was on shift that day—of course she was—and I knew she was the perfect person to carry his physical body to its resting place.

CHAPTER 4

The Maze of Grief

"Life breaks everyone. It's who can put back the pieces."

I'd just handed over my dead son to a nurse and walked out of the hospital.

Even now, writing those words, I still can't believe them.

Did that really happen? Was it a dream?

How does anyone do that? How did I?

I was numb. Not just emotionally — numb in my body, my breath, my being. Moving through the motions like a ghost. I was alive, but without lifeforce. Empty.

I honestly don't remember how I got back to the apartment. I have no memory of that night. Did we sleep? Did we speak? Did I eat?

I don't think I messaged anyone. Craig handled all of that.

Maybe I've wiped it. Maybe my nervous system just couldn't cope with the enormity of it all. Maybe that's what shock does — it protects you from feeling too much too soon.

(That numbness was its own kind of gift. It let me feel less, until I was able to feel at all)

My next memory is being in mission mode. Packing. Organising. Just moving. I couldn't stay in that apartment. I couldn't be near the hospital. I just needed to get out. Go. Anywhere but there. I just wanted to be home.

So, I stayed task-focused. Kept busy. But as we loaded the car, panic hit — fast and hard.

The tears came uncontrollably. My chest tightened. I couldn't breathe properly. I kept looking around, trying to orient myself, trying to find something to hold onto. But there was nothing.

Why was I leaving without my baby?

My body started to shake. I didn't want to get in that car. I hated that stupid car and everything it represented.

How do you drive away from your child?

Somehow, I got in.

Our next stop was the hospital, one last time, to collect Will's things. The nurse manager and social worker met us out the front. I couldn't go back in. I couldn't face those walls. At that moment, the hospital felt like the most painful place on earth.

Now, I see it differently. It was Will's home. The only home he ever knew. But still, I haven't gone back. Even driving near that part of Brisbane sets something off in my body. The tightness. The grief. The truth.

It all comes flooding in.

One day I'll go. And when I do, I want to take Liv.

She's asking more questions now. She knows she had a brother. She knows he was sick. She knows he lived in the hospital.

I want to show her where he lived. I want her to feel his presence. I know I'll be ready. I'll just need a large box of tissues and a deep breath.

When we collected Will's belongings, I hugged the nurse manager and the social worker. Or at least, I tried.

It was a broken hug. I had nothing left to give. It was just the motion of putting my arms around someone — it was the action of a hug with no feeling.

That's what broken felt like. Like your love and energy have been drained out of you. Like you're still standing, but barely.

I just wanted it to be over.

I don't remember her face. I don't remember if she looked me in the eye. But I remember her words.

"Your life will never be the same again."

At the time, they didn't register. But she was right. So right. It would take months — years — for me to understand just how true that was.

—

We arrived home.

It was the strangest feeling — walking through the front door again.

Part of me felt relief. After five long months, we were finally back. My bed. My lounge. Sunshine Coast air. The sound of birds. The green of the trees. There was space again — space away from the tiny apartment, the hospital, the concrete city that had been our life for so long.

But as I moved through the house, the relief started to fade.

There was no sign of Will.
He had never been here.

For a moment, I questioned everything. Had it all been a dream?

The house was exactly how we'd left it before he was born. Untouched. Normal. That's when the panic hit again.

Not tears this time. Not breathlessness. Just that deep, spinning feeling of complete disorientation.

Where am I? What just happened? Was any of this real?

I felt like I was caught in some sort of altered reality again — trying to make sense of something that made no sense at all.

But Will was real.
I did have a son.

I went straight to the bags and began pulling out the photos — the ones my sister had given us in Brisbane, the ones we'd used in the apartment, in Will's little corner.

I started placing them around the house.

Immediately.

Seeing his face, having something of him here — it helped calm me. My breath returned. My body settled.

I do have a son. And now, I could see him here. In our home.

Then the questions crept in.

Had we made the right decision — not bringing him home to die?

How do you ever know what the right decision is when your child dies?

Nothing about it is right. Nothing about it feels okay.

But I still believe, in my heart, that not bringing Will home was the best decision we could have made at the time — for him, for us, for our family.

And that's what matters.

I had no idea what happens when someone dies.

My grandad was the only person really close to me who had passed. He died in a nursing home. We went to his funeral. A few years later, we scattered his ashes at the Anzac Day service at Elephant Rock in Currumbin.

It was sad — especially for Grandma. But he'd lived a good life. And I suppose I just accepted that's how death goes.

This... I couldn't accept.

Death is not meant to happen this way.

Suddenly, there were decisions. So many decisions.

Do you want ink footprints of Will?
Do you want an autopsy?
What does that even involve?
Which funeral company do you want — the one who'll collect your baby's body from the hospital morgue? From the freezer?

Funeral.
I hadn't even thought about a funeral.

What do you do at your son's funeral?

Do you want a viewing? Do you want to see him again?

Of course I did. I needed to. But did I want to see him like that? Would it still be him? Would others want to see him like that?

All I wanted was to hold him again. That need — it was overwhelming. Consuming. It still is sometimes.

It felt like a part of my body was missing.

And then... there was the milk.

My breasts were full. Leaking milk that was meant for my son. My body didn't know he was gone. My hormones didn't know. My whole being was still trying to care for him.

This isn't how life is meant to work.

Children aren't supposed to die.

You're supposed to die first.

I kept clinging to anything I could — teddy bears, pillows — anything soft I could cradle, cuddle, rock. It was instinct. My arms were aching for him. My entire body just had to hold him.

In a strange way, I was lucky.

I got to hold my five-month-old niece, Rosie. She helped ease the pain in my heart, even just a little. Those moments with her — and many more that followed — became part of my healing. I'll always be grateful to my sister for that.

Maybe that's why I still hold Liv so much. Why I never tire of her climbing into my lap or sleeping in my bed.

Because letting go... it still hurts.

My family arrived either that first afternoon or the next day. It was the first time I'd seen them since Will passed.

I could see the pain in their faces. They didn't know what to say or do. And at the time, I didn't really care. I didn't want anyone's sympathy. I didn't want them to feel sorry for me.

What I didn't realise, not then anyway, was that the pain I'd felt watching Will suffer — that helplessness — was what they were feeling for me. Their grief mirrored mine. It was just moulded differently.

But I didn't see that straight away.

When they arrived, I was cold. Stand-offish. I told them I was fine. And that's something I did well — I could act like I was fine. I could hold myself together just enough so people wouldn't see how broken I was inside.

I isolated myself until I felt strong enough to let people in.

But the truth?

I wasn't fine. And sometimes, I'm still not.

That afternoon, my youngest sister Lyndsay said something I'll never forget. She looked at me and said,
"Will's death isn't going to be for nothing. I'm going to change my life."

Lyndsay had battled her weight and mental health for most of her adult life. But that day, she told me there was nothing wrong with her — just poor choices. She was alive. She could breathe. And she wanted to honour that. Because Will didn't get the chance.

My reply?

"Well, do it."

Maybe a little blunt. But I meant it.

The next day, she started.

She began a 104-day wellness challenge in honour of Will. And that small act became the start of something much bigger.

It became #104Will.

A movement. A legacy. A ripple effect.

Even now, it continues to inspire people.

I'm so proud of her. Proud of how she turned her pain into purpose. Proud of the way she honoured my son, her nephew.

(The gift of the will to choose life)

It was more than a challenge. It was a tribute. A gift. And it meant more to me than I could have said at the time.

Organising Will's funeral was another surreal experience.

There were so many painful parts to it, but they were interspersed with these strange, almost magical moments — moments where it felt like I was organising his birthday. Or his homecoming. I still wasn't totally sure what was real and what wasn't.

I'd spent so long visualising Will's first birthday party — how it would be a huge celebration of him making it through — that in some strange way, the funeral felt like I was planning that day. Just... a different version of it.

And somehow, Will's funeral became one of the most beautiful days of my life.

Something I know he had a hand in.
It couldn't have been more perfect.

Everything just flowed. Things fell into place like they were always meant to.

The owner of this gorgeous little chapel in the hinterland — who usually only hosted weddings — made an exception for us. She'd lost her twin grandchildren as babies and had held their service there too. She went out of her way to help.

We found a celebrant who just felt right. Genuine. Present. You could tell she was honoured to be part of it.

One of my long-time mentors — a quantum emotional healer who had also lost a child — read out the letter I'd written to Will in a way that only she could.

His favourite nurses spoke about his cheeky personality.

White Lady Funerals handled everything with such grace, making the whole experience feel almost angelic.

And then came the butterfly release.

One butterfly hovered over Craig and me as we stood by the hearse saying goodbye. It just stayed. Danced around us. Refused to leave.

The first of many signs that Will was still with us.

(The gift of signs — reminders that love never leaves us.)

Next was Will's memorial.

And honestly, I was on the strangest high. It felt more like I was heading to a 21st than a memorial.

I'd wanted Will's service to be uplifting. Something that moved people. And it was.

Of course there were tears.
But there was something else too — such great love and energy in the room.
People were energised. Inspired to live better, love harder, be more present.

So many of my nearest and dearest. So many of the most beautiful people on the planet.

My amazing friend Al put together a slideshow filled with warmth and humour — moments of laughter woven into the heartbreak, like only she could do.

My sisters gave a beautiful tribute, reading out messages about how Will had already inspired people to change their lives. They invited everyone in the room to reflect on how they might change theirs too.

We were flooded with messages afterwards. So much love.

I moved through the room like some kind of hostess with the mostess — chatting with everyone, smiling, holding space.

There have been times I've looked back on that day and wondered:
Why wasn't I grieving harder?

Sometimes I've felt guilty that I enjoyed it. That I came across like a careless mum who didn't love her son enough to fall apart.

But what I've come to realise is —
that was exactly how Will wanted his day to be.

He got me through it.

He wanted his mum to celebrate him.
He wanted joy.

That doesn't mean the road has been easy.
It hasn't.

Craig and I were pretty solid that day. He let me take the lead with organising, but he was there. Supportive. Present. And I felt that.

He even seemed in good spirits for most of it — apart from a few quiet tears during the service.

But, like most events we went to, Craig was ready to leave long before I was.
And, like usual, I went along with it.

When we got home, I was craving affection. I just wanted to curl up with my husband and be held.

But Craig didn't have that available.

Or maybe he did… and just didn't want to give it to me.

Either way, I was starting to feel really alone in my grieving journey.

—

And as the law of physics says — what goes up must come down.

That's exactly what happened in the weeks after Will's funeral. I came crashing down to a low I didn't even know existed.

I was totally lost. The lights had been completely switched off.

I know a lot of people going through grief experience this. It's part of the process, I guess. But knowing that doesn't make it easier.

I was back in a world I didn't feel like I belonged to. Everything felt foreign. Like I was an alien walking the earth. Nothing made sense anymore. The world kept turning — but how was I meant to turn with it?

There were days I was so exhausted — mentally, spiritually, emotionally, physically — that I just couldn't move. I'd lie on the couch, staring at nothing. Dozing in and out of sleep. Sometimes I went to bed and held Will's ashes. Other days, I'd sit on the beach for hours, unable to process anything.

I'd close my eyes and ask him to be close. To let me feel his energy. Just to hold him — even the feeling of him. I stayed there for hours sometimes, waiting for a sign.

And I did feel him.
I still do.

But then the "what ifs" kicked in.
God, the what ifs.

They'd started long before Will was even conceived, and they didn't stop. So many decisions to look back on. So many moments to second-guess. So many situations to analyse.

The "what ifs" can drive you mad.

My rational brain knows there are no what ifs. There is only now. I know that. But sometimes I still think — maybe if I just ask one more what if, maybe I can find peace. Maybe I can make it feel okay.

It's taken a long time to let go of that loop. And honestly, I still go there sometimes.

My higher self knows this was for a greater purpose. That this was how it was meant to be. That Will was a gift.

A Peter Crone quote that really landed for me was, *"Whatever happened was meant to happen — why? Because it happened."*

(The gift of knowing Will taught me this: peace lives in accepting what is, not in chasing what ifs.)

But my physical self doesn't always listen.

I've felt torn between those two parts of me for so long. If I'm really honest… maybe my whole life.

Why are there all these different parts of me?
I just want to feel whole.

All I wanted was to feel normal again. But I didn't. Everything felt different. Everyone around me felt different.

Then I realised — it wasn't them. It was me.

Every time I left the house, I felt out of place. Like people were staring. Whispering. Not sure what to say. And I didn't know how to act.

If I smiled, I felt judged for being too happy, too soon. If I stayed home, I felt judged for not coping. When I tried to go back to work, I felt judged for rushing it. But if I didn't, I felt like I was letting my business down.

Most of those judgments?
They were coming from me.

I wondered if I was depressed.
I wondered if I would ever feel normal again.

--

In those early days, my only outing was to get a coffee at my local cafe.

Everyone there knew what had happened. There was no risk of bumping into someone who didn't know and having to answer impossible questions like:
"How have you been?"
"What have you been up to?"

People just smiled and said hello.

And some days, that was the only interaction I had. The only time I left the house. But it gave me something — a glimmer of normal and in retrospect some connection. It reminded me that I still existed in the world.

It also made me realise the importance of taking the time to smile at someone. Just a simple hello can be a gift. We never really know what someone is going through.

That time taught me to slow down. To notice others more. To connect.

Later, in my studies, I learned about mirror neurons — how our brains reflect the emotions of those around us. Those smiles? They were triggering something in me. Tiny chemical shifts. Little sparks of feel-good hormones.

And when you start getting those small hits of hope, you want to return to the place that gives them. So, I did. That coffee shop became a safe place.

—

But outside that bubble, everything felt meaningless.

I'd scroll Facebook or overhear conversations and feel this rage just boiling up inside me. People complaining about the most pathetic, first-world problems.

Didn't they realise my son had died?

How could anyone care about any of those things?
How had I ever cared about any of those things?

I started to get angry.

Angry at what had happened.
Angry at the world.
Angry at everyone.

There were moments I'd punch the couch. The pillows. The bed. I'd scream. I'd throw things. I'd sob. It was a rage I'd never experienced before.

I was lucky it was mostly contained. It didn't hurt anyone. And it didn't last forever.

But not everyone is that lucky.

Then came the dark thoughts.
The ones you don't want to admit. Not even to yourself.

There were moments I truly believed I was being punished. That I must have done something wrong. That I wasn't a good enough person. That this was my consequence.

And then it would flip.
Hard.

I'd be filled with fury at the world. At all the awful people who seemed to skate through life untouched.

Why did drug-addicted mothers get to have healthy children?

Why did people who neglected their kids still get to keep them?
Why did people whinge about their children — while mine was gone?

Of course, I don't think like that now.

Now, I have compassion for the pain that leads people to those places. I don't judge the way I used to.

I get it now.

But back then, the anger was real.

And then came the days when I just wanted to be with Will.

Not metaphorically.
With him.

I thought the only way to do that was to leave this world.

There was one day — I'll never forget it — when I stood on the hill at Point Cartwright, not far from home. There are memorial plaques there. Some for loved ones. Some for people who had jumped.

I stood there for what felt like hours. Staring out at the ocean. Looking over the cliff. Looking down at the rocks.

Wondering.

Would it be quick?

But mostly... I imagined floating. Letting the ocean take me. Finding peace. Holding Will again.

That urge to hold him — it was all I wanted.
I didn't want to die.
I just wanted to be with him.

And I was willing to do whatever it took to get there.

Then the anger came back.

But this time, it was directed at me.

How dare I think like that.
How dare I dishonour Will's life.
How dare I waste the gift I'd been given — to still be here.

I wanted to shake myself.
Punch sense into myself.

Angela — go live.

Appreciate every last drop of this life.
Make it count.

—

Looking back, I got off the couch and out of the slump pretty quickly. I crawled my way into some kind of purpose. Meaning. Movement.

I was going to have a meaningful life. I was going to enjoy myself again.

In hindsight, maybe it was too soon. I still had so much emotional work to do. But who decides what's "too soon" in grief?

And honestly — how do you even enjoy yourself after something like that?

It felt like a foreign concept. I couldn't remember what joy felt like. How to laugh. How to be light. Even now, it takes more effort than it used to. It doesn't flow the way it once did. But I know it will again.

I caught up with some of my close girlfriends, hoping to feel like myself again. We had a few laughs. A couple of drinks. Moments of how it used to be.

But every time I felt even a glimmer of relief, I was consumed by guilt. It felt like betrayal. Like if I let myself escape the pain, it meant I didn't love Will enough.

I knew that wasn't true. But that's where my mind went.

So much of Will's pregnancy — and his life — was filled with pain and grief. Feeling that pain somehow made me feel closer to him.

And that's a tough bond to break.

Eventually, I turned my focus to work. To my business.

Maybe Will's message was part of my higher purpose. Maybe I was meant to share it.

After pulling out of a speaking event, I decided to send in a video message instead. I spoke about Will. Shared a little of our story. I wanted to help people. I wanted to make a difference.

But then came the guilt.

It had only been six weeks.

What kind of mother does that — works six weeks after losing her baby?
And worse — what kind of mother uses her child's death in her work?

Even though I didn't get a cent for doing it, I didn't want anyone to think I was profiting from Will's life.

It felt like every time I took a step forward, it was wrong.
But staying in the darkness didn't feel right either.

I was stuck.

I didn't know how to move. How to be. How to get back to me — the old me.

Would that ever happen?

In an enlightening Quantum Emotional Healing (QEH) session, I came to a realisation that changed everything: there is no going back to the old me.

As Michela gently said, who I was then had died. And now… it's about rebuilding the new me — with Will's spirit in my heart.

That made so much sense. It gave me permission to stop trying to return to something that no longer existed. To stop pushing to "bounce back." Instead, I could allow the new me to take shape — however long that took. And that was okay.

It was comforting. And it helped me accept and sit with the foreign emotions I'd been trying to outrun. They weren't wrong. They were simply part of the new version of me being formed.

Something else profound happened in one of my first sessions back with Michela. I received a message from Will — as clear as anything — that he was bringing me his little sister. Soon.

The space you're taken to in sessions like this is hard to explain. It's something that needs to be experienced.

All I know is this: it was as clear to me then as it is now.

I was sitting in the most luscious green field, feeling light in my body and glowing with happiness, when Will's energy arrived. It looked like a glowing, bright, angelic light — but it felt like him. Pure. Familiar. I felt his presence completely.

(And yes, I know this might be getting a bit weird for some people.)

He let me know he was okay. Happy. Doing his work. Letting him go had been a gift that needed to happen. And that's when he told me Liv would be here soon.

As soon as I came out of that session, my mind flooded with objections. All the reasons it couldn't or wouldn't happen. But he was right.

She did come.

—

One thing that brought a smile to my face during those tough days was the ripple effect of the 104-day challenges that had started to emerge after my sister's wellness challenge for Will.

Not only was she becoming a healthier, more grounded version of herself — people were starting to ask how they could do one too. When I saw others joining in, it felt like Will's life mattered. Maybe that's what he was here for.

It gave me a burst of energy. Another glimmer, this time of purpose.

That's when we made it more official. It became #104Will.

These challenges had a wellbeing focus and often supported a charity component. But even so, promoting them still stirred guilt in me — and sometimes it still does.

Long before Will, my work had always been about inspiring others to live healthier, more intentional lives. One area I used to speak on — before Will was conceived — was stress management.

But I often carried this uncomfortable thought: What if I'm a fraud?

Not because I didn't believe in what I was teaching. Not because I didn't live it. But because I hadn't really known stress. I hadn't had the pressures of kids, financial instability, serious illness. I didn't feel like I'd earned the right to talk about stress when I'd never been through the storm.

Well... the last few years have given me a relentless cascade of stress. So that's no longer an issue.

But sometimes I've wondered:
Did I attract this?
Did I somehow cause my son to go through everything he did just so I could prove something or release a belief I didn't even realise I had?

Was I using Will's life to fulfil some unconscious need?

Promoting #104Will began to feel like self-promotion. And then the guilt would spiral.

It's taken a long time — and a lot of therapy — to untangle that.

One of my mentors said something that helped me turn the corner:
"Destiny has chosen you. And if you don't start spreading Will's message, you're doing yourself, Will, and the millions you could help a disservice."

That advice helped shift something in me. It helped me reach a point — almost — where I could begin sharing #104Will without shame.
It's also part of what led me to write this book.

I'm so glad I got over myself enough to complete my first #104Will challenge. Because there was a miracle waiting at the end.

I set two intentions for that first challenge: do some form of yoga every day, and laugh every day, for 104 days.

I had to learn how to laugh again. And it wasn't easy.

Some days I'd reach the end of the day and realise I hadn't laughed at all. So, I'd go searching for it. My go-to was Ellen clips on Facebook or YouTube. And 99% of the time — they worked. I managed a laugh.

And on Day 104?

I was 103 days pregnant.

After years of trying, after IVF, after so much grief… I was pregnant. Naturally.

The gift of Liv was on her way.

The news of my pregnancy with Liv was one of the most pivotal moments in my healing. It gave me hope. Hope that joy could return. That there would be light again.

And while I could already feel my marriage beginning to drift — fears creeping in about what might fall apart — this was the one thing I hoped I wouldn't lose.

Focusing on the higher purpose of why some bad things may happen was how I coped in the beginning. It helped me survive. But looking back now, I can see that I may have tried to move forward too quickly. I leaned into purpose as a way to avoid some of the deeper emotional pain—especially the anger and the guilt.

Those emotions didn't disappear. They waited. And eventually, they surfaced in ways I couldn't ignore.

In the early days, I used whatever I could to move the energy—crying, venting to friends, scribbling in a journal, even punching pillows when the rage got too big. It wasn't polished. But it helped me survive.

Over time, I discovered other ways. Deeper ways. I worked with truly magical healers with all different specialities, immersed myself in modalities that helped me not just release pain—but integrate it. Let it shape me, without consuming me.

The guilt has been the hardest. I still have moments where I blame myself. My waters broke—that's the fact. Will needed my waters intact to form his lungs and survive. And although I've been told again and again, through healing sessions and even spiritual messages from Will, that it wasn't my fault, there's still a part of me that holds it.

I don't know if I'll ever fully let that go, but I've made peace with the process of trying until I hear about something else that might help it go away.

And I feel lucky. Not because of what happened—but because I had the knowledge, support, and tools to find my way through. Not everyone does. Grief can break people. It can consume them.

That's part of why I'm writing this book. Not to say "here's how you fix it." But to say: You're not alone. You're not broken. There is a way through, even if the path is messy and non-linear.

Grief doesn't end. It softens. The waves come less frequently—and then sometimes, they come crashing again. And that's okay.

You don't get over it. But you do find a way to carry it.

(To carry grief is to carry love. And that carrying love is what makes life worth living)

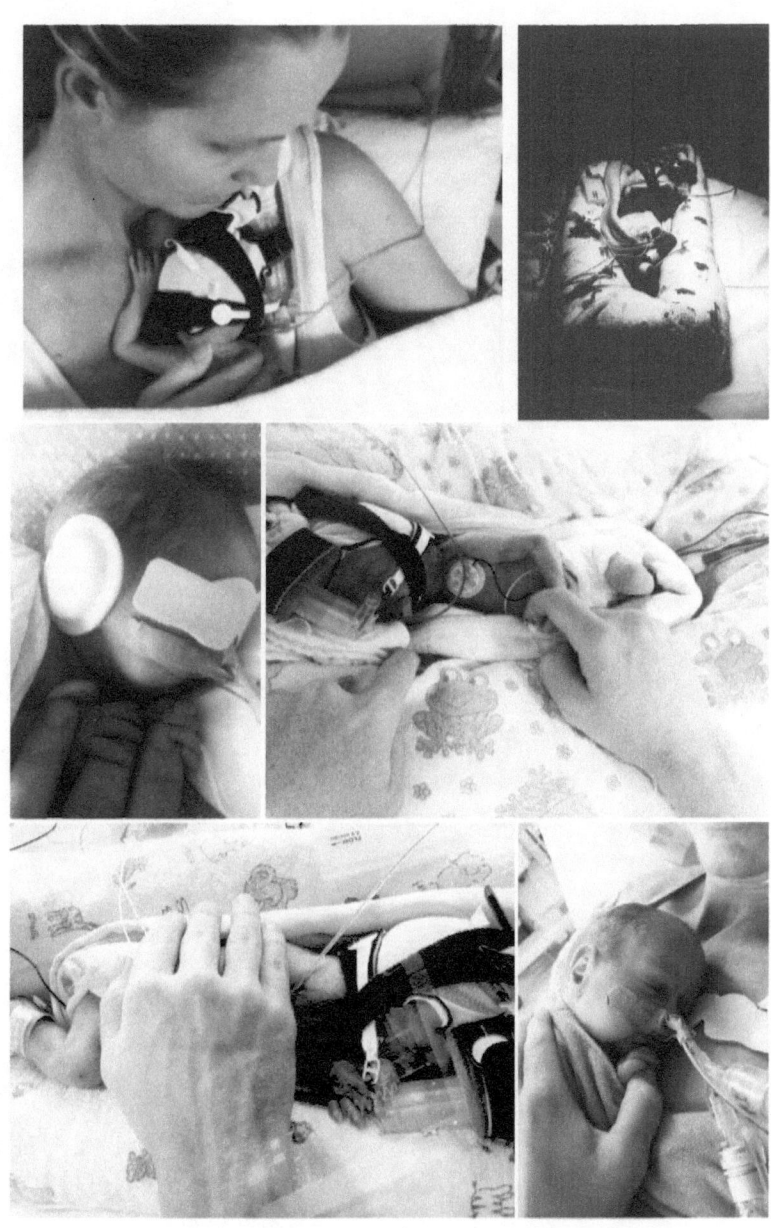

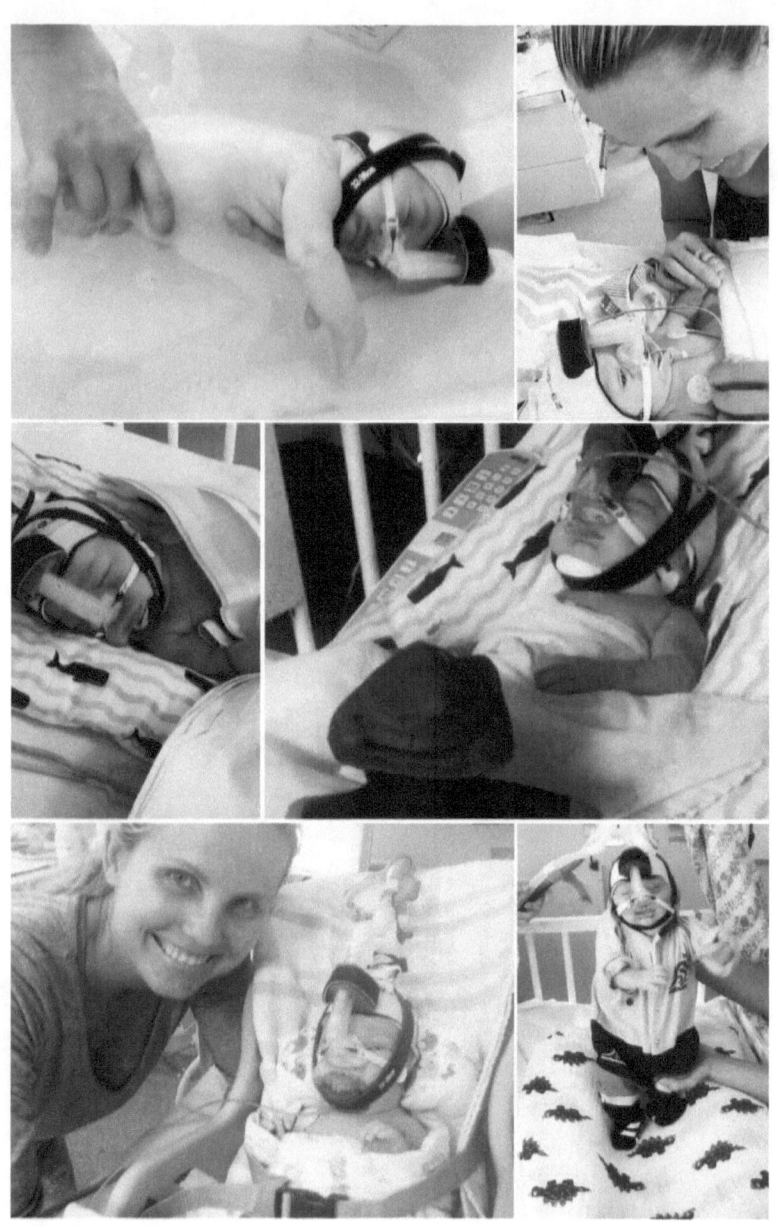

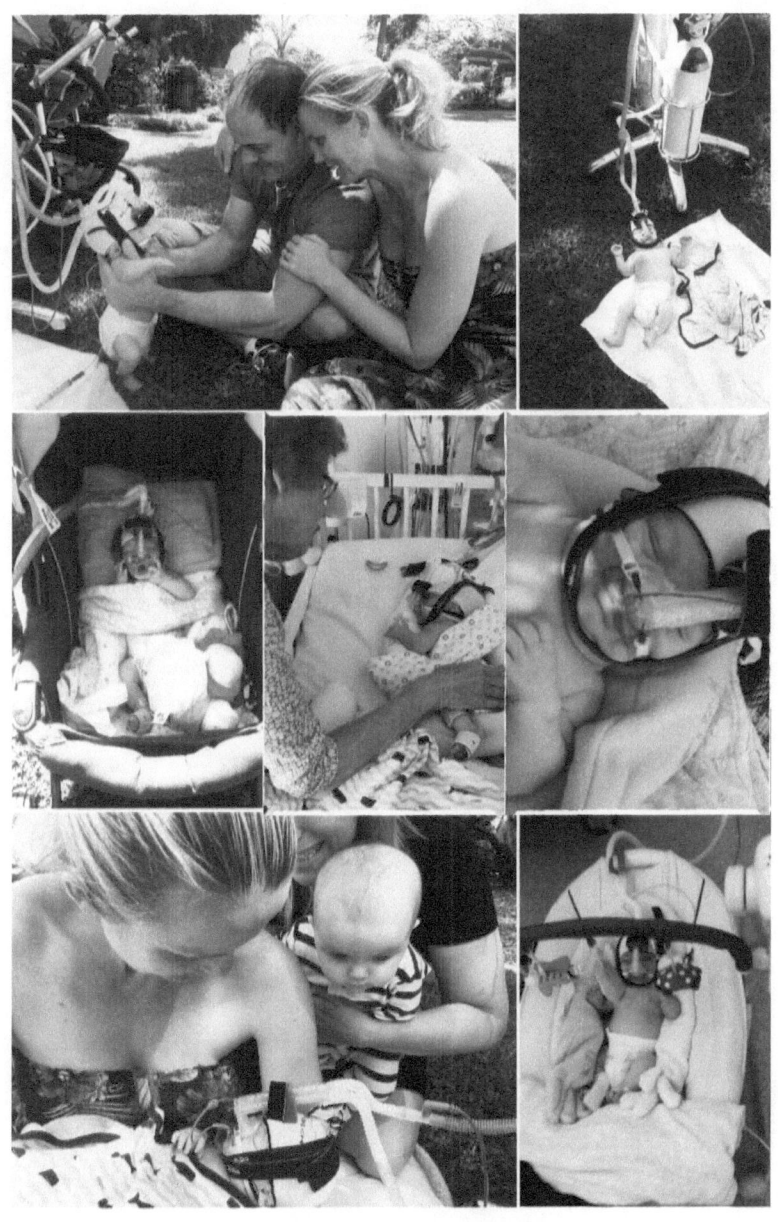

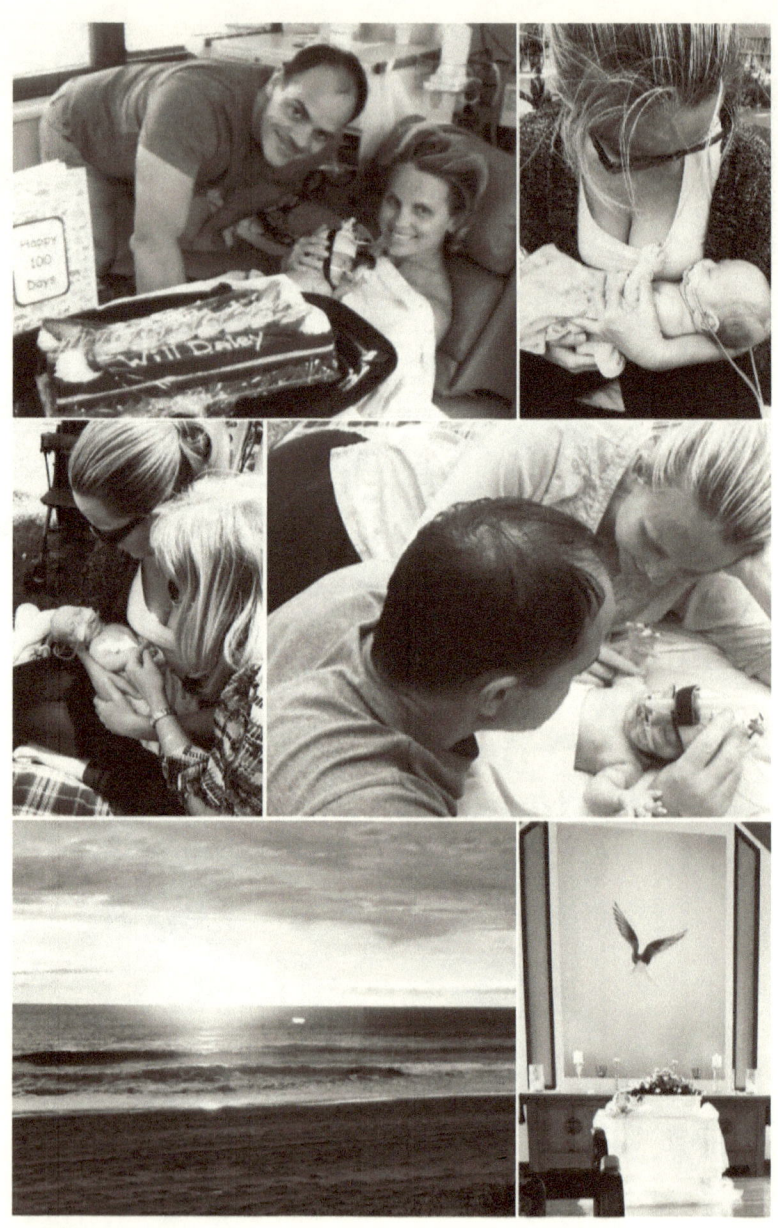

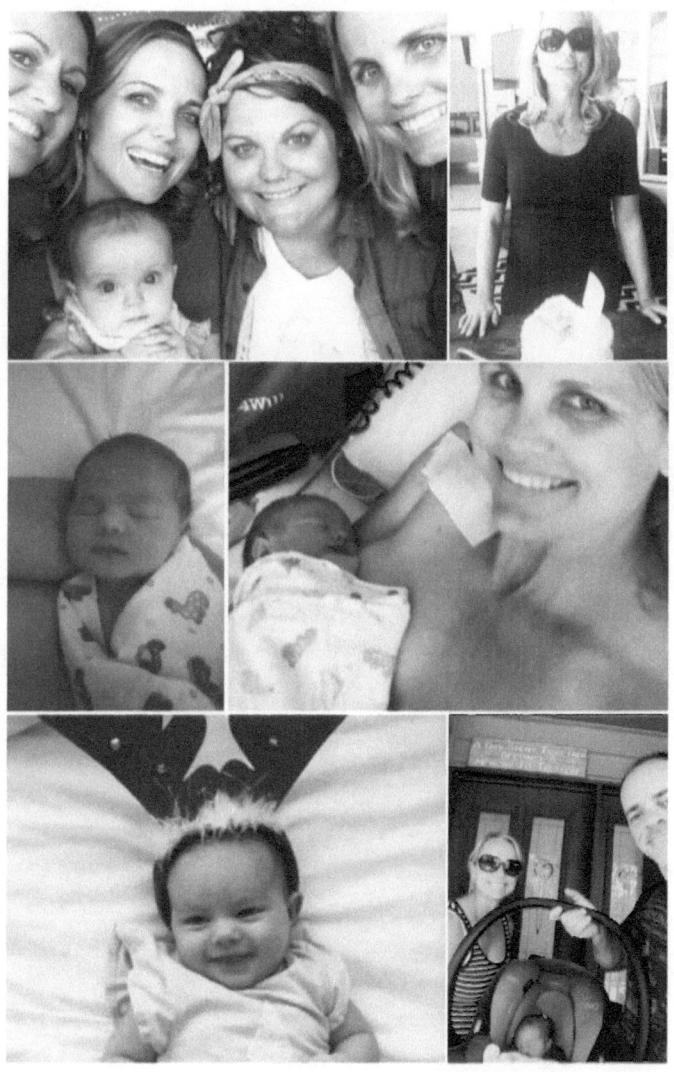

PART TWO

THE

HEALING

CHAPTER 5

The Ripple Effect of Trauma

"Post-Traumatic Stress or Post-Traumatic Growth"

Trauma doesn't just affect you—it ripples into everything and everyone around you. Since losing Will, my entire world has shifted. Relationships have changed. Friendships have deepened or drifted. Business dynamics shifted. And my marriage... it didn't survive the storm.

I've done a lot of reflecting, trying to make sense of it all. Some things I can understand. Others are simply beyond me—and maybe always will be.

We often talk about how becoming a parent shifts your values. Suddenly, there's this tiny human you're responsible for, and nothing feels the same. But losing a child? That kind of shift is next level. It tears through you, right to your soul and changes how you are wired. For me, that transformation was rapid, intense, and relentless. It was like life hit fast-forward with no time to catch my breath. I gave birth to Will. I lost Will. I gave birth to Liv. All within just over twelve months. And then 12 months after that I was a single mum selling up the life I had dreamt of for so long.'

Everything turned upside down.

And I mean everything.

The career I had poured myself into for years—my identity, my ambition—plummeted down the priority list. I was trying to make space: for Liv, for Craig and for the painful hole that grief had broken open.

What I've come to realise is that there are a couple of core reasons why so much around me changed. And the first one starts with me.

Everything—on some level, reflects who we are and what we value. And I wasn't the same anymore. I valued different things. I was starting to live differently. And when you shift from the inside out, it's only natural that the people and environments around you shift too.

The second thing is this: trauma affects people in wildly different ways. We each carry grief in our own time and through our own lens. There's no rulebook. No right or wrong.

But what I didn't expect—what I couldn't have prepared for—was how my trauma would stir up other people's grief. My breakdown unearthed things they'd buried. For some watching me grieve, watching me unravel—it triggered things in them that hadn't yet been healed.

And sometimes, when people aren't ready to face their own pain, they can turn away from yours.

What's been hardest for me to sit with is this feeling that I've tried—really tried—to own my part in the relationship changes... and feeling like others haven't.

But maybe I didn't always get it right either. Maybe I didn't try in the way they needed me to. Maybe they did try, in ways I couldn't see or feel at the time. Maybe it was all just part of us being human —and not meant to last in the way it once was.

I've had to come to terms with the fact that some relationships may never find their way back. Some people just don't have the capacity. Maybe I didn't have the capacity to hold that relationship any longer. Or the timing wasn't right. Or maybe our paths simply diverged when the road got hard. Or maybe we have simply outgrown each other and who knows may reconnect one day.

(Sometimes we need the space created from letting go.)

I think about one relationship that hurt me deeply for a long time. Every time I tried to express how something was affecting me, I was met with deflection or denial—phrases like, "Be careful how you're perceiving that," or "You should've told me." And in my heart, I know I tried—gently, clearly, repeatedly.

What I needed wasn't defence. I needed empathy. The willingness to sit with discomfort. To listen without fixing or justifying. And I wrongly or rightly had the expectation that this person was capable of that or 'should' of been capable of that.

But maybe they just weren't ready for that. Maybe they still aren't.

Even though my mind understands that, my body held onto that pain for a long time. It settled in my cells, it was heavy, another layer of hurt. One I felt could have been prevented.

(Reading this back now, it feels so small in the scheme of things — but the hurt I carried then was very real. That energy was intense, and it stayed inside me until I shook and breathed it all out!)

That realisation—that I wasn't just grieving Will but grieving who I'd been—brought me face-to-face with something bigger: the mirror of relationships.

With relationships, there are always different expectations, different values, different capacities for communication—and, I've learned, vastly different levels of emotional readiness. And for me it felt there was just so much stuff coming to the surface all at once to deal with.

Sometimes, I think people are brought into our lives not just for love or connection—but to show us what still needs healing. They reflect back the parts of ourselves we haven't dealt with. And when we avoid that healing, the same lessons resurface again and again, dressed up in new people and situations. Sometimes in disguises you never see coming until you're already in it. Just when I thought I was making progress something else was revealed.

Looking back, I've been love-bombed, manipulated, betrayed, lied to, controlled, and taken advantage of. But I also see now— none of those things would've had the same power over me if I had loved myself more deeply, valued myself more fully, and held stronger, clearer boundaries.

That's not to excuse the actions of others—but it is to own the part of me that stayed quiet, that tolerated what didn't feel right, that didn't listen to those whispers, and that thought being loved meant being needed. Those lessons didn't come easy, but they came for a reason.

And when grief comes, it comes in hard and fast. And in doing so, it reveals who we are at our core. I saw the best and worst in others—and in myself. What I've come to learn is this: it doesn't matter how many books you've read, how much personal development work you've done, or how mentally strong you think you are. If there are wounds from childhood still buried inside you, trauma will find them. And when it does, its game on.

We all have a choice when that happens. We can face the shadows—those uncomfortable, buried parts of ourselves—or we can run. I've chosen to face mine. But not everyone does. Not everyone can. Still, grief and trauma will find a way to bring them to the surface. That part is inevitable.

In a strange way, I now see it as one of Will's many gifts to me – post-traumatic growth, not just post-traumatic stress.

When I zoom out and look at all the situations that came to a head—conflicts, shifts, breakdowns—I can see now that I was the one staying silent. The woman I was back then didn't speak up when things crossed my inner line. She accepted less than she deserved because part of her believed that she had to prove her worth to be loved.

But that silence? That self-betrayal? It became the shaky foundation everything was built on.

(The gift of self-worth — learning to hold my own boundaries.)

People assumed I was okay with certain things because I never said otherwise. So, when I finally did find my voice—when I finally said "this doesn't work for me anymore"—some people couldn't hear it. They weren't ready. Or maybe they were never able to. They liked agreeable Angela. It made them feel good.

As the saying goes from hermetic texts 'as within, so without; as above, so below'. If I was betraying myself, if I wasn't trusting or believing in myself, then of course I attracted relationships that mirrored that. This deeper understanding helps me explain not excuse the different things that unfolded. And that means I can take responsibility for my part—and leave the rest to them.

Your trauma and grief really does ripple out to the people around you. Some didn't know what to say. Some were amazing. Some did their best. Some disappeared. I often found myself wondering: Did anyone truly understand what I was going through? And really, how could they?

Unless you've held your child as they took their final breath, handed them over to the nurse and shut that door forever you can't fully know. People might imagine it. They might touch the edge of it. But most haven't lived it.

And yet—this experience gave me a new understanding of grief and trauma in others. It made me look back at the people in my life with new eyes. There were times I feel I wasn't a good friend. Times I didn't know how to support someone in pain. I just didn't get it.

But now I try and do better. When you know better, do better. That insight has helped me soften—not just toward others, but toward myself too.

A term I came across that really resonated with me was that of *compassionate latitude*. An understanding that most people including me are doing the best they can with what they've got.

And maybe, just maybe, it's time I let myself off the hook as well.

—

The ripple effect on my work was a big eye-opener for me.

For so long, my business wasn't just a job—it was my identity, my purpose, my first baby... until I had a real one. I poured over 20 years into it, heart and soul. Because I gave so much of myself to my work and the people in it, I expected that same emotional commitment in return

But as Don Miguel Ruiz reminds us in The Four Agreements: Don't make assumptions.

I thought I understood that concept when I first read the book a decade ago. I nodded, underlined, highlighted. But it wasn't until I lived it—until I lost Will—that I truly got it. Assumptions don't protect you. They set you up for heartbreak.

I found myself going around in circles, trying to work it out. Was I too emotionally entangled in my work? Did I over-identify with it? Was I in the wrong environment altogether? Or did I just not understand the people I was in it with?

If I'm honest, all of the above are probably true.

Over time, resentment built. Not just toward the business—but toward myself. I was angry that I had prioritized work so heavily over the friends and family who showed up for me, no matter what. They were there for me during the darkest nights of my life. My business wasn't. And yet... was it ever meant to be?

Can a business really hold you after you've just held your son as he takes his final breath?

Of course not.

And yet, I still expected it to. I expected emotional support, understanding, compassion. But businesses aren't designed for grief. They're built for growth, results, strategy. I was looking for something it couldn't give.

Once again, my expectations had betrayed me. I used to think having high expectations was a strength. And maybe it still is—but only if you can detach from the outcome. Expect nothing. Give everything. Let go.

Piece of cake, right?
Yeah, not exactly.

Still, I did come to realise something important: work will always be a part of me. I love what I do. I care deeply. It's not just work—it's purpose. It's passion. But now, I go about it differently. I operate from a higher place. One that's more aligned with who I am and why I'm really here. The grief gave me that clarity. The loss gave me that truth.

I'll always want to help inspire others, to make an impact. But now I do it from a place of fullness, not depletion (well I try to most of the time!). I've learned that giving without receiving isn't this higher level of yourself—it's dangerous. It only works if you're first giving to yourself.

And like everything else in this chapter, this too had layers. Could the business have supported me more? Could they have responded differently when I brought up the unbearable grief I was carrying? Could someone—anyone—have stepped in when behaviours crossed the line?

Yes. To all of it.

But just like the relationships in my personal life, it's not about right or wrong. It just is. The experience was what it was. They kept moving in the way they knew how, while I was forced to stop and face everything I'd been avoiding. And still, I chose to keep showing up, sacrificing, hoping something would shift. I'm grateful for the great years – the growth, the opportunities, the people who did cross my path through that work. But I can also see now that throughout my whole working career I had stepped far beyond my own boundaries, abandoning myself in the process.

But I've slowly reclaimed that power.

Letting go of a business I once loved more than anything created space—real space—for the two great loves that remained: Will and Liv.
It hurt like hell, but it gave me back something I didn't know I'd lost—my own energy, my sense of purpose, my voice.
It's one of the many unexpected gifts Will has given me.

So yes, I was the one who let it affect me.
I was the one who got tangled up in it.
But I was also the one who chose to let it go.
And that choice has become one of the most empowering things I've ever done.

—

Another realisation I had in the months after losing Will was that people show love in their own language—not necessarily the one you need or want.

Some people took it head-on. They asked the hard questions. Others lit up Facebook with support or quietly completed

#104Will challenges without ever saying a word to me. Some I hadn't seen in years gave me heartfelt hugs in the street. Others sent gifts. They were all trying, in their own way.

And I appreciated all of it.

But for the people closest to me—my inner circle—I had a different bar. I needed more. And when they didn't show up in the ways that mattered to me, it felt like they hadn't shown up at all.

What made it harder was that, for many of the men in my life, their way of supporting me was mostly through doing things—acts of service I wasn't even always aware of. I needed connection. Words. A hug. A moment of shared emotion. And I didn't get that. I felt completely let down.

I've since come to realise that they were showing up in their own way. They were trying a lot more than I realized or gave them credit for.

The other truth was that the emotional door wasn't just closed with these men—it was sealed shut. They didn't know how to hold space for pain. They didn't know how to stay in the discomfort. They ran. Buried their heads. Shut down. It was all too hard.

And before anyone says "that's just men," I want to be clear—I don't believe that. I know men who are capable of deep emotional expression. But I also know how ingrained the pressure is for men to suppress, to fix, to stay strong. I feel for them. But I also don't accept that it has to stay that way.

I see now that I played a part in it too. I've been fiercely self-sufficient most of my life. I rarely showed my vulnerabilities or let anyone see how deep the pain really went. And if you don't let people in, how can they show up for you?

Still, I hope I can get to a place where the disappointment doesn't hurt as much. I've let go of so much already. But there are moments—unexpected ones—when it still hits. When the wounds feel fresh again. Forgiveness, I'm learning, doesn't always arrive all at once. It comes in layers.

—

Grief has a way of circling back, even after you think you have let things go. Just when I thought I'd released enough, it was like here we go again. This time getting into the deeper layers. Once the dust of the initial shock began to settle, things I hadn't even realised I was holding onto started to rise. And true to my Type A nature, I didn't tiptoe around any of it. I faced it head-on. One of the most unexpected emotional eruptions was with my dad.

Will's death triggered so much anger in me. Old pain, old questions, old grief. You see, my parents separated when I was nine. I'm the eldest of three girls, and though Dad had some involvement in our lives, he eventually moved away. And I couldn't make sense of that—not after what I'd just been through. How could someone willingly step away from three healthy daughters, when I would have given anything—anything—to have just one more moment with my son?

That pain hit me hard. And in the weeks after Will passed, I didn't hold back. He told me not to. I said what needed to be said. And to his credit, my dad stood there and took it. He didn't run. He listened. He accepted my words, my truth. And something changed between us.

We talked. Really talked. I learned more about his own story. Understanding his past hurts did help me reframe mine. I began to see the patterns. The inherited wounds. And also, the strength that came from them.

Because while his absence left their scars, it also moulded the women my sisters and I became—strong, independent, resourceful. That's part of his legacy too.

And these days, our relationship is better than it's been in a long time. I'm learning to hold onto the gifts. Seeing him as a Grandad to Liv is one of them.

But the biggest ripple of all—the one that changed everything—was in my relationship with Craig. Our grief journeys didn't just look different - they went in completely opposite directions. It's as if when Will passed away this giant fork appeared in the road, and we started walking in different directions. And the further down we went, the further we drifted apart.

There just wasn't enough room. Not for both of us. Not for the grief that was consuming us. My cup was already bursting. I was barely holding myself together. Every bit of what I had left I was pouring into our beautiful little girl making sure she was ok.

Could I have made more room for him? Maybe.
Could he have made more room for me? Maybe.
Would it have changed everything? Maybe not.
But I do believe it would've changed something.
And that still hurts.

(The gift of truth may break things apart, but it always sets you free.)

—

And yet, even in the middle of all the breaking, there were lights that kept me standing. Two people who spoke my language—and who became two of my greatest shining lights through all of this—were my younger sisters.

They showed up for me in ways I didn't know were possible. They held space, hugged me when I couldn't speak. I honestly don't know how they knew what to do. It certainly wasn't from me—the big sister who moved away straight after uni and left them while Mum was still recovering from her brain tumours. If anything, I'd modelled distance, not closeness.

Another thing I would have done differently.

But somewhere in the middle of my grief, they stepped in with a kind of compassion and empathy I now realise I hadn't always given to them—or to anyone, really. What they gave to me; I now want to give back. To them, and to others. Before Will, they were my sisters. After Will, they became two of my best friends.

And then there was my mum. Just by being my mum, by existing in that mother space, she held something solid for me. Something that didn't require words.

I was also held—really held—by a circle of women. Some close, some unexpected. Women who checked in, sent messages, laughed and cried with me, sat with me through whatever arose and just listened even when I had nothing left to say. They didn't need to fix me. They loved me for who I was – for who I really am. They were just there and are still there. That mattered more than they'll ever know, and I feel blessed to be doing life surrounded by amazing soul sisters.

The ripple effect of trauma didn't just expose wounds—it revealed goodness. Kindness. Strength. Strangers, friends, colleagues, people I hadn't spoken to in years... they showed up. In words, in actions, in quiet gestures that made me feel less alone.

I've seen the best of the human spirit rise out of the darkest places. I couldn't possibly list them all without doing someone an injustice. But to those of you who offered your light during my darkest moments—thank you. I believe every one of those gifts will return to you tenfold.

(Love is all around.)

CHAPTER 6

For Better but Not for Worse

"Every little thing gonna be alright"

Author's Note

During the years after losing Will, Craig and I went through a separation and, eventually, a divorce.

In the original draft of this chapter, I let it all out. It was a vent — an honest, unfiltered account of what happened after losing Will, and how grief changed the dynamic between Will and Liv's dad and me.

Writing it was important. At the time, getting those words out helped me process some of the hardest emotions I'd ever faced. Later, when I revisited it from a calmer and higher perspective, I could see there were still truths worth telling — and lessons in how relationships shift after the loss of a child.

But at this final stage, I've chosen to keep those details private. Despite everything, I want to honour Will and Liv's dad and leave space for his own journey, without my words shaping how others see him. He lost his son too.

This story is about Will, and about love, resilience, and faith. And even though life isn't perfect right now, I still believe what I held onto when Will was in hospital — that every little thing is going to be all right.

I know I could write a whole book about the breakdown of my marriage — and maybe one day I will. But not here. This isn't that story. This book is for Will. For Liv. For the light they've both brought into my life. And that's where I want to keep the focus.

(The gift of honouring my children above all else.)

CHAPTER 7

The Light of Liv

"My Rainbow Baby"

Liv Jenkins.
A year — to the very week — after losing Will, my greatest gift arrived. His little sister, my rainbow baby. And it's Liv. Not Olivia. Just Liv.
Her name means exactly that — "to live." To live your best life.

From the start, Liv's life has been surrounded by miracles and synchronicities that still make me feel how destined she was. The message from Will in a quantum emotional healing session, telling me his little sister was coming soon. The fact I was 103 days pregnant at the end of my first #104Will challenge. That she was born in the anniversary week of Will's passing. And, after years of fertility treatment, how I somehow fell pregnant naturally.

Despite these signs — and my deep knowing she was a miracle — the guilt crept in, especially in the early days of Liv's life. It visited for a long time. Liv is here because Will isn't. If my pregnancy with Will had gone to plan, she wouldn't be here. Some people say maybe she would have come along later, but the odds of me falling pregnant with a two-month-old in my arms are pretty slim. It's one of those "what is, is" truths — maybe part of the grieving process.

Most of the time, I'm celebrating her life, knowing that celebrating her also honours Will's. He's part of her, part of us. But the guilt had a way of sliding in through the cracks for a very long time. On a rational level, I get it. On an emotional level, it's more stubborn. That's where acceptance comes in — letting the feeling be there without letting it take over. And then, of course, feeling guilty about feeling guilty.

The pregnancy with Liv, to be honest, couldn't have been more perfect. No complications. She measured in the top percentiles the entire way through, and I was healthy. The hardest part wasn't physical — it was managing the fear. I didn't want to give that fear too much energy, in case I somehow manifested more tragedy. But after what had happened before, I couldn't quite believe I wouldn't be unlucky again.

I often told myself, surely this pregnancy can't go wrong. I can't be that unlucky twice. But I'd been there before. The reality is women can go through terrible pregnancies more than once — and many do.

All you can do is control what you can, be present, and try to enjoy what's here right now. Angela, are you actually starting to wake up and listen to some of your lessons??!! Well... kind of.

In those early weeks, I was living from a place of fear. I tried to detach completely from the fact I was pregnant — as though keeping my distance emotionally could protect me from getting hurt. I wasn't connecting to the baby growing inside me at all.

Then I remembered something the midwife had said when Will was born: "No matter what happens, you WILL always have a son." The same was true now. No matter what happened, I would always have created this baby. Something in me shifted. I felt the connection just fall into place, and I loved her with all my heart from that moment on and still do more and more every day. I knew she was a girl. I knew she was special.

There were so many scans, check-ups, and milestones. We were in the clinic almost every week. Reaching 12 weeks was huge. Then 24 weeks — a 'viable' baby. Then 28 weeks — a third trimester Will never reached. Then 30 weeks — the survival odds soared. And finally, 38 weeks — delivery day.

Because of my classical caesarean with Will — the vertical incision into a more fragile part of my uterus — labour wasn't an option. Going into labour risked a rupture that would have been dangerous for both of us. So, we planned a caesarean. I didn't care about how my little girl was being delivered, every part of me just wanted to hold a healthy baby.

The morning of her birth felt so surreal. We checked into our private hospital room — like a hotel suite, but instead of browsing the compendium and raiding the minibar, I unpacked photos of Will on the bedside table. I wanted him there with us, part of our family.

The staff knew our history. The midwives, anaesthetists, and our obstetrician, James, were extra cautious, extra kind. They kept reassuring me with every little thing they were doing and what was happening. I didn't want to talk much. I kept my eyes closed, focusing on my breath, focusing on staying calm and praying.

Craig was beside me, holding my hand. James talked us through each step of the operation, his voice was so calm and steady. Then, within minutes, I saw her — arms outstretched into the bright theatre lights as if she was embracing life itself.

"Is she okay?" I asked, even though I felt she was. I just needed to hear it. And she was. She was okay. My daughter was okay.

She let out a big, strong cry. Breath. Life. My baby was alive.

Craig held her first. Then she was wrapped and laid on my chest. She was home. I was home. In that moment, every ounce of fear, grief, and anxiety left my body. I cried and cried and cried — happy, relieved tears. The complete opposite of the tears that had filled the last 18 months.

Holding her was the purest joy I had ever felt. Feeling her breathe easily against me — after so much time focusing on every strained breath Will took — was a blessing I'll never take for granted. Breath is life. And that moment meeting my little girl has been the greatest gift of my life, one I will forever thank Will for.

The first few days in hospital were such an eye-opener — not only in the sense of having a newborn, but in seeing how different this experience was compared to Will's. I'd only ever known Will's start to life, so I hadn't seen the other side. The side of having a healthy baby.

With Will, nurses and midwives monitored him 24/7. Now, without all that constant intervention, I was beginning to realise something so obvious: Liv was well. She was healthy. She didn't need all those wires and machines.

Another shock was how freely I could pick her up and move about the room with her. In those first couple of days, there was a moment when she was crying and wouldn't settle. I sat beside the cot, my hands cupped gently over her — the way we had been taught to touch Will. That was all we were allowed with him: still, cupped hands. Movement could cause him stress and make breathing harder.

A midwife came in, saw me, and simply said, "Just pick her up."

Of course, you just pick up your crying baby. That's all I had wanted to do with Will but never could. Yet somehow, in that moment, I hadn't realised I was allowed to with Liv. I picked her up, and she settled instantly.

(The smallest gestures can be the greatest privileges.)

That small moment floored me. I began to realise just how different things had been for Will — how far from "normal" our first experience of parenthood was. In the moment, I'd normalised it. I'd had no reference point. Now, I felt like I was in an emotional storm, being thrown between joy, grief, gratitude, and guilt.

When I picked Liv up and held her freely, my mind went straight back to the pain and suffering Will endured. The pain and suffering I had consented to for the hope of keeping him alive. The guilt was there again, sharp as ever.

Looking back now, I can also see I was in denial about the state of Craig and my relationship. I wanted to believe we were happy, because I wanted our family to be happy. That's all I had dreamt of. But even in those first days with Liv, there was an undercurrent of tension that I hadn't expected. Craig had moments of reacting very differently than he had before. It's only been with time that I've realised no one can truly take away your happy moments — but sometimes, life's dynamics can make it harder to fully hold onto them. I've had to learn how to protect those moments and let go of any resentment.

One of the biggest moments came when we popped Liv in the carrier and walked out of the hospital. It was surreal to have the freedom to do that. I kept looking around, almost double-checking it was real. I wasn't ready to sit in the front seat. I sat beside her in the back with my hands on her just to make sure she got safely home.

I was overcome with emotion when we walked through the front door. We had finally brought our baby home.

During bedrest and those long weeks in NICU with Will, I'd closed my eyes so many times and pictured that exact scene. I had prayed for it. Visualised it so clearly, I could feel it. And now, 12 months later, here it was — except I had to consciously remind myself that the baby in my arms was Liv, not Will.

—

The first few weeks were a sleep-deprived blur — me trying to work out what the hell to do, as is the case with most newborns — but they were also the most precious of my life. Most of our time was spent on the couch, breastfeeding, just me and Liv in our little bubble of love, staring into her big brown eyes.

I once watched a beautiful video that described what it's like for a newborn coming into the world — the colours, the smells, the sensations, the touch of the person they've been tucked up inside for nine months. They come out in awe of the beauty of the world. The beauty of life that we, as adults, so often take for granted.

I thought I'd been good at appreciating things before. I'd kept gratitude journals, taught the practice to others. But often, once the ten or twenty minutes of writing was done, I'd rush on to the next thing on my list, missing the beauty around me. Will had reminded me of the fragility of life and how little time we have. Liv was reminding me of its beauty.

It started with me watching her facial expressions as she experienced things for the first time. Now it's her waking up and saying, "Mum, it's morning!" — happy simply because we've been given another day. Or the time she said, "Mum, let's go and watch a beautiful sunrise. They are so beautiful." I hope she keeps that wonder and doesn't get numbed to the experiences of life like so many of us do. I know I have to be mindful not to dull that spark for her.

In those first weeks, I loved catching up with family and friends, sharing moments that felt long overdue. I could feel their joy — they'd been on this journey too, felt the heartache, and now celebrated this chapter with me. And yet, as had been the pattern since Will passed, every time I felt joy, I'd stop myself and make sure I was thinking of him.

I needed him to be part of these happy times. I needed him to know I hadn't forgotten, that I hadn't just replaced him with another baby. One baby dies, I don't just "get another one."

So, I started another #104Will challenge — 104 photos and journal entries, celebrating small moments with Liv and consciously thinking of Will there with us. At first, it helped ease the guilt. I could feel him with us — sitting in the garden, Liv's feet in the ocean for the first time, feeling rain on her skin, listening to the birds, her first family holiday at three weeks old to Aunty Kristy's wedding.

But over time, the joy turned to pain. It became too much. There was so much happiness around Liv, but it often came with an undercurrent of sadness, reminding me of everything Will didn't get to have. The inner conflict was tearing me up inside.

(Grief doesn't leave when joy arrives. They just live side by side.)

I know you can't live life constantly thinking of "what might have been" — not in this dimension, anyway — but even now, writing this, I'm reminded that I want to finish that challenge and keep celebrating the small things with both Liv and Will, who is always with us.

I'm also mindful that I never want Liv to feel she's living in Will's shadow or that she missed out on my love because I was still grieving. One of my energy mentors has told me it's good that I've been able to open my heart and love Liv fully. I hope that's true. She has lit up everything around me since she arrived. Life has been lighter, brighter, because she's in it.

I want her to know how precious she is, how much she's brought to my life. She's beautiful, caring, compassionate, cheeky — the best daughter anyone could ever wish for. And I wished her into this world. She's brought such a healing energy that I can't imagine life without her. The thought takes me to a dark place I don't want to go.

From the very beginning, if I cried or got upset, she'd burst into giggles — the best healing medicine. As she got older, even at the grand age of three, she'd hug me, ask if I was okay, and once even wiped my tears away with a sarong. I don't know if it's good or bad that she's seen me cry. For most of her life, it's been just her and me, so it's inevitable. I want her to know it's okay to feel and express emotions, but I also hope she's not carrying my pain.

When she was almost two, nearly a year into my life as a single mum, I received a letter from her first daycare teacher. It spoke of her empathy and how caring she was as a friend. I know I shouldn't need outside validation, but it gave me a boost. It was my very first teacher feedback, and I hope she carries those qualities with her as she grows.

—

There are so many decisions we have to make as parents. My brain often feels full of the daily choices I need to make for Liv — choices I make day in and day out, often on my own. How do you ever know if you're making the best decision for your child? I've realised there aren't always clear rights or wrongs, but there are always consequences. Every cause has an effect, and every effect has a cause. All I can do is live with the outcomes, and try to make my choices consciously, not on autopilot.

My experience with Will has helped me do that. I often wonder what kind of mum I'd have been if I hadn't had him first. I'm naturally impatient — the kind of person who wants tomorrow today — but with Liv I've found a patience and calm I never expected. Not always (let's be honest), but most of the time. I believe that's one of the gifts Will passed on to my parenting.

I think it stems from pure gratitude. Gratitude that Liv is happy, healthy, and alive. Will's lungs were so damaged, and his vocal cords affected by the ventilator, that we hardly ever heard his voice. So, every cry that kept me up at night, every tantrum, every screech from my little chatterbox — I've welcomed them. Who could be annoyed at a healthy set of lungs?

When we were in hospital with Will, some of the highlights were simple things like getting to give him a rare bath or change his nappy. Craig and I would take turns because we both loved doing it. So changing Liv's nappy feels like a privilege — a stinky privilege, but a privilege, nonetheless.

I've also spent more time simply enjoying her. I know first-hand you can never get those moments back. Nothing is permanent. Every time I get caught up with work, Will and Liv bring me back to centre. When she says, "Mummy, come and sit with me on the couch," I don't need to send that email. When she says, "Mum, that's enough working," it's enough.

It's something I've reconnected with more recently — starting each day by enjoying each other. It began with me adding some breathing and music into my mornings when I felt flat, and grew into us dancing, laughing, and starting our days in joy. Some mornings we put on full shows; other times she lines up her dolls and teddies as the audience. I love it when she wakes up and says, "Let's get up and do dancing, Mum."

I even make it a priority in my planning — I draw a reminder in the centre of my weekly to-do list. You'd think I wouldn't need a reminder to be present with my daughter, but it helps.

One of the other big realisations since having Liv is the irony of all the situations I once judged. In a session with one of my mentors, she pointed out that one of the lessons Liv is teaching me is non-judgement — of myself and of others. These kids we love more than anything, who can also be little rascals, are the best teachers.

Pre-Will, I had all of these "I'm never" rules:

"I'm never having a caesarean."

"I'm never doing IVF."

It's funny now. Anyone holding those judgements should feel the longing of someone desperate for a child. That wish, that gift, should be honoured no matter how it arrives.

Since my mentor pointed it out, I've laughed at myself for many of my other "I'm nevers":

"I'm never using a dummy." That lasted three weeks.

"I'm never having a glass of wine until I finish breastfeeding." Then reality set in — sleep deprivation and a newborn are relentless. A glass or two (timed with the help of an app) was a welcome treat. Cheers.

"I'm never putting my child in front of the TV just to get something done." The Wiggles, Peppa Pig, and Elsa have been my saviours as a single mum with a toddler.

"I'm never bribing my child with junk food." This one lasted longer, until a supermarket tantrum ended with me handing over chocolate (70% dark chocolate so I will give myself some grace).

"I'm never sending my child to daycare." At 16 months, Liv started daycare. Partly because I needed to work, and partly because I needed some time for me. It's been amazing for both of us, and I now have zero judgement for any parent's daycare choices.

I'm sure there will be plenty more "I'm nevers" to come.

(Our children are often our greatest teachers — especially when we think we're teaching them.)

I keep coming back to my "bible," The Conscious Parent. It's a constant reminder of how I want to be and how I want to parent Liv. It's about her, not me... funny that. We are all unique (someone I know bangs on about that in her work), and I hope I can truly understand Liv's uniqueness as she grows — not shaping her into what I want her to be, but supporting her to discover what is best for her.

I suspect a few "I'm nevers" will pop up here and there, because it sounds so easy on paper.

One of the book's biggest lessons is that our children are here to teach us. The very things that frustrate us are often mirrors of what we still need to heal in ourselves. So, when I see Liv being a bossy, knows-what-she-wants little soul... well, I have to admit, I might recognise a bit of myself there. Maybe I'll just keep focusing on how funny, kind, and caring she is.

It's both amazing and confronting to realise that the patterns Liv forms up until the age of seven will drive most of her subconscious behaviour for the rest of her life. (Don't panic if your kids are older — patterns can be changed.) In these early years, she's a sponge, and the energy I bring as her primary carer is the number one thing that will shape her. I heard Brené Brown say something like that once, and it cut through the noise of all the parenting advice out there. It gave me one clear focus: choose the energy I bring, and how I show up.

This is where I've realised, I need time for me. I'm not invincible. It doesn't mean I love Liv less — it means I need to fill my own cup so I can love her more.

There are days when my energy hasn't been my best. Parenting is relentless — tantrums, tears, "No! I said no!" on repeat, food and mess everywhere, being part waitress, part chauffeur, part cleaner. And yet, in the middle of that, there's love. There's her first "I love you, Mummy"... and then, not long after, her first "I don't love you anymore, Mummy" when she didn't get her way. Kids keep you humble.

We've had our arguments and our frustrations. I've wondered when it will get easier, whether I'll ever go to the toilet in peace again. But then I remember how quickly these years pass. Before I know it, she'll be off to school, and my little buddy who's been by my side will be in a classroom.

Most of the challenges come when my cup is low. And it has been low at times in the past few years. But I'm the adult — it's my responsibility to manage my emotions and my responses, not hers. I do it much better now. And yes, sleeping through the night and her being able to get her own snack from the fridge helps.

Through it all, one of the things I love most is how aware Liv is of Will. One day she pointed to his picture and simply said, "Will." My heart melted.

On her second Christmas, she picked up a decoration my sister had made with Will's photo on it and said, "My brother Will," hugging it to her heart. She's taken that ornament out with us before, insisting Will ride in the back seat, and has even "shared" chocolate eggs with him — which somehow ended up in her mouth.

We've taken Will's photo magnets to the beach and set him up on the towel. These moments seem to happen around special times — Christmas, Easter, Mother's Day, my birthday — and sometimes just when I'm a bit sad. It's his way of letting us know he's with us.

(Children carry wisdom we can't always see — they feel truths our adult minds forget.)

Sometimes his presence is so strong I'm certain he's in the room. I often wonder if Liv can see or feel him in a way I can't.

She knows he was in hospital and that he was sick. When she plays doctors and nurses, she talks about caring for him. She talks about him being "up in the stars" and points him out when we look at the night sky. Sometimes she says she can't wait to give him a cuddle on his birthday.

Just last night, as I was writing this, she got upset out of nowhere. We hadn't spoken about Will in a while, but as I dressed her for bed, she started telling me how much she missed him, her eyes filling with tears. Then the sobs came — big, heaving cries — as she said she wanted to cuddle him and touch "tiny Will." She took his photo from my bedside table, held it to her chest, and kissed it. She climbed into my bed with it, snuggling in as she cried.

I climbed in beside her, holding them both — my daughter and the picture of my son — and cried too. In that moment, I realised she knows and understands so much more than I'd thought. She feels his absence. She feels my pain. She's likely felt her dad's too.

It was beautiful, special, and heartbreaking all at once. I don't know how I'll navigate that as she gets older. All I know is that Will is with us and will always be a part of Liv's and my life. Family is what you make it, and this is ours.

A Note from Now

As I write these final edits, it's six years later. Liv is in grade three, on the cusp of turning nine, and I can hardly believe how quickly my little girl has grown into this tall, strong, soulful being. She's right on the edge of the tween years, yet she still carries that spark — that light — that has been with her since the moment she was born.

We've shared so much in these years — school events, birthday parties, trips away, fun times with family and friends, and all the little in-between moments that make up a childhood. I've soaked up every milestone and hope I've been your biggest cheerleader — I've certainly tried. I don't regret for one second putting other parts of life on hold to be that mum. The years have brought their challenges, of course, but they've also brought countless moments of laughter, adventure, and joy.

There have been times when Will hasn't been as present in our everyday lives — not because we've forgotten him, but because life has been full and we've been busy living it. And yet, he's always with us, in ways big and small. Sometimes I see him in you — in your eyes, in your smile, in the way you sometimes say the most profound things beyond your years. You carry his light forward in ways you don't even realise.

Liv, I am so proud of who you are, just for being you. I love the way you show up for your friends — how you notice when someone needs a kind word, how you stand beside them when they're having a tough day. I love your curiosity, your cheekiness, and the way caring for people, animals and nature just seems to be part of who you are. That awareness, that empathy, and that love are gifts.

If these years have taught me anything, it's that the everyday moments are what truly make a life. Not the milestones, not the achievements — but the small things we share, because those small things are actually the big things.

You make me laugh, you make me come alive, and you remind me daily of what matters most. You are my rainbow after one hell of a storm, and the brightest light in my life.

I could write a whole book about you, Liv — and one day, maybe I will. For now, I'm just so grateful for every hug, every sunrise, every giggle, and all the mummy-and-Liv adventures still to come.

CHAPTER 8

Coming Home

"The Will to Liv Starts Now.."

The number of times I've heard people say that their worst nightmare would be if anything ever happened to their child, or that they couldn't go on if they lost one, is too many to remember. I think it's because it's everyone's fear.

Even now, that fear is still mine. If anything ever happened to Liv… the thought alone makes me physically sick. I can't go there.

So, what do you do? How do you go on after holding your child as they die—and being the one who had to make the decision to let them go? Is it even worth going on?

All around the world, right at this very moment, families are losing children—some in ways far more horrific and violent than mine. *(Not that grief should ever be compared.)* Mums and dads are suffering the most painful wounds imaginable, wounds so deep they never truly heal. Many fall into a spiral of depression so dark that their lives collapse and never get rebuilt.

I once listened to a podcast by parents who had lost their child in a mass school shooting in America. They described the hole in their hearts — a hole that would never go away. I understood that, because I carried one too. But they also said this: if you grow your heart bigger with more love, the painful hole becomes smaller by comparison.

And I've found that to be true. Yes, I had a wound beyond imagination — but I also carried Will's spirit, his strength, inside me. The life I live now isn't just for me; it's for him. Because in part, it is him. We are one.

In fact, in those early years after Will, when Liv was little, I was constantly searching for ways to make sense of what I was living through. Most nights, after she was asleep, I'd be up late reading books or listening to podcasts about mental, emotional, and spiritual growth. I devoured anything I could find—teachings, tools, stories from others who had walked through their own darkness.

That included everything from neuroscience, ancient traditional practices and exploring the mysteries of quantum physics. There were so many voices that influenced me in ways I can't even name, but what I know is that each one planted a seed. At the time I didn't realise it, but all that searching was slowly reshaping me from the inside out.

The biggest realisation for me was understanding that I was now a different person. I felt it at a deep level, but I questioned it a lot—especially as many people around me struggled with the "new" me. When something changes inside you, things change around you.

One of my mentors put it perfectly: When Will died, who you were died too. And that's exactly how it felt. I couldn't be the same person.

And so many of the things I identified with before were no longer relevant. The dominoes fell—Angela the centre owner, the business partner, the wife—all gone. Along with the family home and the businesses.

And in their place came new, almost unbearable identities: single mum to a newborn, and… a mother who has buried her child.

Everything I thought I was had been stripped away. So, who was I now?

The answer, I would come to learn, was not about going back to the "me" I had lost. She was gone. This was about rebuilding and becoming me—the real me—for the first time in a long time.

Who was I?

In my 30s, I lost myself.

It wasn't sudden. It kind of just happened slowly. It's something I didn't realise until this journey. Somewhere along the way, I decided that growing up meant becoming a different person. The free-spirited, fun Angela started to fade, replaced by a more serious, responsible one. My focus shifted to the outside world, and somewhere in the process I lost sight of my inner one.

So much of it was about external validation—something I can see so clearly now.

I came back from London at 29, full of stories and freedom, but then I looked around and saw friends buying houses, getting married, "settling down." And I thought, right. That's what I need to do.

Time felt like it was running out. I needed to find a husband, buy a house, and start a family. I decided to rebuild my business too—this time with a team—so I could step back when I had a baby.

I thought I was doing what I was "supposed" to do. But ticking boxes didn't fill me up. The material things weren't bringing the fulfilment I imagined. Neither were the relationships around me. How could they?

You can't have a healthy relationship if you're not whole and true to yourself. And back then, I wasn't.

Looking back now, I can see how the energy I was putting out—and my relationship with myself—was determining what and who I attracted into my life.

It's been a tough road, and I know it will always be a road of learning and enlightenment in the most wonderful ways. One of the most profound gifts Will gave me was this: becoming the truth of who I am.

I feel incredibly lucky to have had the chance to find myself again—unlike so many others who struggle to recover and spiral downwards. Another big reason I'm writing this. I want to shine a light on the path ahead, not just for parents who've lost a child, but for anyone who has lived through hard times, experienced grief, or felt stuck.

Everything I had done before Will—my work, my study, my courses, my professional development—prepared me more than I realised. It had opened my eyes to different approaches, different ways of healing. And more than that, it had given me a deep belief in the human ability to heal.

I believed I could and would get better. The pain had to ease. No matter how unbearable it felt, I knew there had to be something I could do. And so I did it.

I share this because I want people to know there is a way out of pain. There is hope. There is a way forward. Joy can return. Pain can ease. This too shall pass. There is always a way through.

Where there's a Will, there's a way.

Humans are complex. I'm complex. But sometimes, what I've learned is this: healing doesn't always have to be as hard as we make it. If we choose to allow it, it can come with more ease.

For me, there were many "Angelas" to rebuild: Angela the mum. Angela the businesswoman. Angela the friend. And Angela the woman.

And within each of those Angelas, there were four parts: the physical me, the mental me, the emotional me, and the spiritual me. Every one of those parts needed to heal.

Healing in Layers

Rebuilding Angela the mother and Angela the businesswoman came faster than I expected. But rebuilding Angela the woman... that took time. Deep time.

She was the one most broken.

I didn't just need to heal from losing Will — I had to strip away the old parts of me that no longer fit. And in their place, I had to let in new ways of living — ways that felt true to the woman I was becoming.

Traditional Therapy

My healing journey began in the most traditional way: with a referral to a psychologist named Amanda. At first, she helped me process what had just happened, but before long, our work reached far beyond grief. With her support, I began navigating not only the loss of Will, but also the strain in my marriage, the reality of being pregnant again, and the raw, confusing identity of becoming a mother for the first time…. again.

Amanda guided me through practicalities I couldn't see on my own and held space for emotions I couldn't yet name.

Work & Purpose

My work became part of my healing, too. Supporting others through their own challenges reminded me that I still had something to give, even when I felt so empty inside. Helping others helped me. Seeing so many of my amazing clients be inspired to live and love more, if only a little bit by Will's legacy, has supported me back to living. In fact, this book is part of that healing—it's both a tribute to Will and a way of living into my purpose.

I've also come to understand that purpose itself is a fundamental psychological need. It isn't just about having goals or work to do; it's central to our wellbeing. When we have a sense of purpose, we feel anchored, connected, and able to keep moving forward—even through heartbreak.

One of my longest-standing clients, Ginera, is a beautiful reminder of that. I first met her while I was still in the NICU with Will. I remember Skyping into a mentorship call from the hospital hallway, and there she was on the other side of the screen. Ten years later, she's still with me. And although she has technically been my client all that time, I know that walking alongside her—lifting her up—has lifted me up as well.

Body & Movement

Movement has been in my life for as long as I can remember, and in my darkest days it became my most loyal friend. It wasn't just exercise — it was medicine.

Some days it was as simple as a ten-minute walk with Liv in the pram. The difference between the way I felt before that walk and after was like night and day. Without that outlet, I'm not sure how I would have coped with the extremes of anger and hurt that lived in my body. Emotion really is energy in motion, and moving my body gave those emotions somewhere to go.

Yoga became another anchor. Not the perfect 90-minute studio classes, but home practice on my bedroom floor. Often it came with tears soaking the mat, or with Liv crawling over me mid-pose. During my pregnancy with her, those sessions became our quiet time together, a way to connect before she even arrived. And now, watching her do her own little downward dogs and child poses… I feel proud knowing it's a part of her world too.

I learned how unresolved emotions get stored in the body — changing not only our structure but our hormones. That realisation made me want to keep my body as open and healthy as possible, not just for me and Will's legacy, but for Liv.

I worked with one of the world leaders in movement, Ian O'D, to release the fascia — the body's great storehouse of emotion. The techniques were subtle, but the shifts inside me were anything but. I also used a vibration plate to clear inflammation and waste, adapted my exercise to fit the "new me," and found ways to make movement joyful again.

TRE — Trauma Release Exercises — became another powerful tool. By triggering the body's natural shaking reflex, I could release deep layers of stress from my nervous system. And sometimes I would shake simply to music in my living room, letting the tension fall away minute by minute.

There were days when all I could do was place my hand on my heart, breathe in for four, out for four, and remind myself that I was still here. Even that was enough.

Mindset & Emotional Shifts

Rebuilding meant facing the rawest emotions — the abandonment, betrayal, and hurt. In the early years, I was fuelled by anger and resentment. Over time, and with a lot of practice, those feelings gave way to more love, more compassion, more centredness in myself.

I studied the science of happiness, learning amongst other things that only 10% of it comes from external circumstances. The rest is an inside job. On hard days, that sounded impossible. But over time, I understood — happiness is a choice we make, again and again and again.

Epigenetics taught me that social connection is a major driver of my health. My body thrives on oxytocin — the hormone of trust and connection. In times of stress my instinct was to retreat, but knowing this helped me reach out when I most wanted to hide.

I learned to shift my mindset from fear and worry to gratitude and appreciation. To trust that things would be okay — or maybe even better than okay.

Spiritual & Energy Work

My spiritual body had been silent for a while, but eventually it called me back. I worked with two extraordinary healers, Dea and Michela, who guided me through shadow work, shamanic-style healings, and deep emotional releases.

Dea was with me for the next eight years, a constant in my healing, and I know I wouldn't be who I am today without her. With Dea, I learned to speak my truth to those who had hurt me — not by reliving the wound, but by naming what I would have preferred instead. It was liberating. She helped me trust my intuition again, to make decisions from a heart-centred place, and to find neutrality with people I'd once held so much charge toward. Those and countless other gifts will transcend lifetimes.

(Dea – Your love and lessons will be spread out in the world.)

Michela walked beside me into the shadows—calling out truths, reflecting my blind spots, and holding a space of pure love so I could face the parts of myself I wanted to hide. In the quantum work I did with her, I came to realise that a healing I had experienced years before falling pregnant with Will was in fact preparing me for what was to come.

In that earlier session, I saw a past life where I had a son named Will who went off to war. I carried the guilt of not stopping him, of losing him. But in the healing, I understood that he was always going to go—that his path was his own—and that my role was simply to let him go with love. My final memory of him in that life was not of the loss, but of the love.

Looking back, I see how that healing gave me a deeper capacity to let go of my Will. It didn't erase the pain, but it gave me a way to honour him with love as he left this world.

From other teachings, I learned that all behaviour is either an act of love or a cry for love, and that the only thing lacking in a relationship is that which you are not giving. Those truths shifted how I saw myself and others.

I also explored practices that moved energy through my body in ways my mind could never unblock. Shamanic breathwork with Patricia became a powerful tool — guiding me into altered states where my body could release what words and thoughts could not reach. I experienced physical and emotional releases that bypassed the mind entirely, tapping directly into the emotions and pain held in my body.

Another turning point was a Kundalini dance series I committed to. It was as if each movement unlocked a new layer of me — shaking loose old patterns, reigniting joy, and reconnecting me with a flow I hadn't felt in years.

I had read about Kundalini awakenings — the idea of opening up the dormant energy at the base of the spine — and while I can't say for certain, I believe I experienced one.

One day, my body began to shake uncontrollably, as though something deep within me was being set free. Afterward, I felt an ability to move that energy through me in a way I'd never known before. Interestingly, the months that followed were marked by six months of chronic pain — which, in hindsight, I believe was a deep cleansing process. It was as if my body was clearing out years of stored tension, grief, and heaviness so that I could step into a lighter, freer way of being.

--

Even with all the tools, practices, and progress I'd made, there came a day when everything felt like too much.

Every area of my life seemed to be demanding more than I had to give. I'd faced challenges before, but this time the weight felt different. Heavier. More final.

I remember walking to the beach because I didn't know what else to do. I sat on the sand and let the tears come — and come they did. I couldn't stop them.

I'd tried everything I knew to shift the heaviness. Nothing worked. And in that moment, I had nothing left to fix or control or push.

So, I asked for help. Not from a person — but from something greater. The universe. God. Will. I didn't care who was listening.

And then… I felt it.

It wasn't dramatic. It was subtle but undeniable — like being wrapped in an invisible blanket I hadn't realised I'd been craving. An energy wrapping around me that said, you are not alone. You are held.

The relief was enormous. The lightness that began to rise in me was the kind of knowing you can't explain. I realised I had been pushing, searching, and striving so hard — when the answer was here all along.

That day taught me what surrender really is. Not giving up. Not abandoning my life. But releasing the illusion that I had to do it all on my own. Trusting that something greater was already carrying me.

The Journey Back to Intimacy

Rebuilding the woman in me wasn't just about healing my grief — it was about reopening my heart.

In the beginning, intimacy felt impossible. My body remembered the pain of loss, my heart remembered betrayal, and my nervous system braced for abandonment. It felt safer to stay closed. I told myself I was protecting Liv, but really, I was protecting me.

Over time, there were moments — fleeting connections, little flings — that reminded me I was still capable of attraction and desire. After years of pain, it was nice to feel pleasure. The pendulum needed to swing back. But they weren't my person. And I learned to be okay with that.

It's taken years of self-work — physically, emotionally, spiritually — to feel ready to let someone see me fully again. That self-work has included everything from learning self-love and tantric lessons, to soul-mate breathwork courses and practices that pushed me to expand beyond my comfort zone. Everything was on the table. Bit by bit, I wasn't just healing my wounds, I was reclaiming the parts of me that longed for intimacy, pleasure, and connection.

I've come to understand that intimacy isn't about finding someone to complete you. It's about meeting as two whole people, choosing to witness each other.

That doesn't mean I never feel lonely. I do. There are still nights where I just crave for connection, where I cry and wish someone was just there to hold me. But I no longer confuse loneliness with emptiness. I know now that I am already whole.

Until my person arrives — and I do believe he's out there — I'm content with the intimacy I have with myself. I know my worth. I love the woman I've become. And when love comes, it will be an expansion of that, not a replacement for it.

Healing Ceremonies

Years into my healing journey, I felt called to something deeper. I had rebuilt my life in so many ways, but there were still depths of my heart I hadn't yet reached. That's when healing ceremonies found me, with Nanda and Michelle — two women whose wisdom and presence opened doorways I hadn't known were there.

I entered these ceremonies surrounded by people I trusted, in spaces held with safety and intention. This wasn't about escape — it was about truth. I'll never forget turning up nervously to my very first ceremony. As I walked in, a young man I'd never met, approached me with a gentle smile. 'Hi, my name is Will,' he said. My body relaxed instantly. I knew, in that moment, I was exactly where I was meant to be.

In those journeys, I've felt an unconditional love I didn't even know was possible. Not just an emotional warmth, but a soul-level love — the kind you can't put into words because it's beyond them. I came to see that we are all made of that pure love, every single one of us, and that the only thing that clouds it is the layers of our own pain.

I've connected with Will there, not just in memory, but in an understanding of his journey — why he came, why he left, and how his short life could create ripples that help others live from their hearts instead of their heads.

There have been profound realisations about Craig, too. I've been able to see him from a place of love, even if the reality of our interactions hasn't changed. I've released old patterns that once kept me in cycles of pain. In some ceremonies, I've felt as though I was helping to heal the pain of generations before me — including my great-grandmother, who lost a baby but was never allowed to speak of it or even visit the grave.

The ceremonies have shown me what an evolved relationship could look like — the kind of love and partnership I want to attract. It has also shown me clearly the mum and woman I am and want to become, and the leader I am growing into.

And it has taken me into even deeper surrender. Not the one-time moment on the beach, but an ongoing practice. A softening into trust. A returning to the knowing that life isn't meant to be forced into shape. Now, every time I catch myself pushing too hard or gripping too tightly, I come back to surrender — not as giving up, but as choosing to be held by something greater than myself.

It's been beautiful and confronting all at once. But more than anything, it has helped me remember who I am — a woman wanting to live with an open heart, connected to something greater, and committed to living from that place for the rest of her life.

I came home to myself.

Living the Legacy

This chapter isn't about a happy ending. There's no bow tied on grief, no finish line for healing. But there is peace. There is love. And there is me — rebuilt, real, and finally home inside myself.

Everything I've lived through has brought me here. To this voice. To this mission. To Will to Liv.

Will gave me the greatest gift of all — he gave me my will to live. Liv gave me the gift of living.

And now, I choose to honour both of them: by showing up in truth, by living a life filled with meaning and joy, by helping others remember that no matter how dark it feels… there is always a way through. Because where there's a Will, there's a way.

And that's what I want you to carry from these pages: the Will to Liv isn't a distant hope. It isn't something you wait for. It's a present choice. It begins here. It begins with you.

The Will to Liv starts now.

Closing Reflection

The woman who first started out writing this story is not the same woman who is editing it now, ready to send it out into the world six years later.

When I began, I was still in the thick of my grief — very raw, very fragile, and trying to make sense of a life I never imagined I'd be living. I was writing to survive, to get the pain out of my body and into words.

Now, as I finish, I see it differently. So much has happened in these years. I am not who I was then – and thank goodness. I thought I was rebuilding, but the truth is, I had already arrived. Even in my brokenness, even when I couldn't see it, I was already enough. It's the paradox of life — that we have arrived while always still arriving.

Editing these pages has been its own kind of healing: revisiting the hardest moments, seeing how far I've come, and recognising the love, resilience, and meaning that were there all along. Now I can finally see it.

This book began as a way to share Will's story — to make sure he was remembered and that his life, though short, created ripples that reached far beyond his 104 days. I hope it has done that and more. His legacy is here, in every page, not just to tell my story, but to help you live yours more fully.

If his life can remind you to slow down, to love harder, live more of you, fill your life with what matters most and to know joy never leaves you even in the hurt — then Will's purpose continues. That is the heart of Will to Liv.

I came home to myself. And my hope is that through Will's story, you find your own way home — and live the life that's waiting for you.

And now, it's time to raise a glass — to Will, to Liv, to love, and to life.

Cheers

THE END

Appendix: The #104Will Challenges

Some people live their lives by yearly goals, others by quarterly reviews, and some by lifetime dreams. For me, life is now measured in blocks of 104 days — because for me, that is a lifetime. It was Will's lifetime.

Since he passed, I've already lived through so many of Will's lifetimes in my own years. And I'll be honest — so many of them slipped by when I wasn't truly living. I was disconnected, unhappy, unsatisfied, and nowhere near living my purpose or potential.

Don't get me wrong, I haven't lived a life of complete misery. But I am learning to live differently now. And every 104 days, I'm reminded to return to this path — to live fully.

Will's 104 days have become a reminder not just for me, but for my loved ones and many others: wake up and appreciate the gift of life. Because yes, life is a gift — one that's taken too soon for many, and one that's often unappreciated by those who still have it.

I've had to ask myself painful questions: If I'd been more grateful for my life, would I have needed to go through such loss to learn the lesson? Would Will still be here?
I can rationalise the answers and not get stuck there, but the waves of blame are part of what I live with.

In Will's 104 days, the only breath he ever took was his last. Every other breath came from a machine. Think about that. Breathing is something we don't even notice, yet some people never get the chance. Breath is life. Maybe we all need to pause with our next breath and simply give thanks.

Some people are born with genetic conditions or disabilities that make every day a fight to survive. Most of us, however, are born healthy — and yet we make choices that destroy our bodies. It's not until health is gone that we realise its value.

The Rise of #104Will

Will's life became a wake-up call for my sister Lyndsay, who began the first #104Will challenge. What started as a wellness reset became her reclaiming her entire life. Looking back at photos, she wonders where she'd be now if she hadn't shifted paths. She has since inspired so many others to take on their own 104-day challenges — improving health, building gratitude, and changing destructive patterns.

The shift toward gratitude really does change everything. Instead of filling the void with energy drinks, sugar, alcohol, or comfort food, people begin to feel fulfilled. Gratefulness becomes a lens through which we nurture our bodies, our choices, and our lives.

It wasn't just Lyndsay. Will's great-grandma Doris, at 87, set her first #104Will challenge: daily breathing exercises. Once a champion swimmer, she now lives with emphysema. She decided that while she still had breath, she would honour it. Years later, she still hears Will's reminder: do your breathing exercises. It's never too late to shift focus and improve your life.

Others committed to losing 10.4 kg in 104 days, to giving up smoking, alcohol, or soft drink — asking, why destroy my lungs when Will never got the chance to use his? Some set fitness goals: from never running at all, to completing 10.4 km, to one incredible man running 104 km simply "because he could."

For some, Will's legacy meant family. One family completed 104 training sessions together; another made 104 family outings.

A stranger who never even met me was so moved by Will's story that she organised an event with 104 people dressed in blue, running 10.4 km together. She gave me a sign I now carry to my talks:

"Thanks for joining us today... because you can."

Such a simple message. So powerful. (*Thank you Kylie E.)*

Challenges of the Heart

Six weeks after Will passed, my touch football team entered the NSW State Cup in his honour. I wasn't in shape after bedrest, trauma, and loss — but the girls wanted to play for Will. They wore blue wristbands and, with tears streaming down our faces before the final, we played as one. Somehow, hobbling and exhausted, we won. I even scored a try — rare even in my best years. That weekend, filled with laughter, tears, and teammates, was healing in ways I can't explain. #roosters

Other challenges grew from there. People booked holidays of a lifetime. Some like my beautiful friends Anita and Kim climbed mountains — 104 of them. Anita began journaling each climb of Mt Coolum, where her father's ashes rest. Each ascent gave her time with him and a new perspective.

Children joined in too. My girlfriend Billy's six-year-old son Kobe set himself the challenge of doing 104 kind acts. He wrote them down, one by one. Not long after, he won a kindness award at school. That's the ripple of Will.

Another mother and son decided on 104 fun things together. Their life had been full of barriers, with the son living with an intellectual disability. But through this challenge, they created joy and memories they thought they could never have.

My friend Kylie marked her challenge with permanence: a tattoo on her forearm. For her, it's a constant reminder to appreciate life. She's found new ways to love and live — spoiling Liv along the way as her "other aunty."

There were many, many more challenges — too many to mention here. But please know that each one, no matter how big or small, helped spark my light back to life.

From Personal to Global

Businesses picked it up too. Many in the fitness industry ran 12-week challenges because it was the done thing. Inspired by Will, they shifted to 104 days. Suddenly, clients weren't just "getting through a program." They were living a lifetime. One coach even designed a full 104-day workbook themed around Will's legacy.

And what's remarkable is that most of these challenges evolved naturally without me knowing. People simply felt it.

Now, I see a vision: people across the world committing to 104-day challenges to enrich their lives. Fitness programs. Personal resets. Family goals. Acts of kindness. Breath. Gratitude. Love.

Not because it's trendy. Not because it's about money or charity (though many have raised funds for NICUs and causes close to their hearts). But because life is short. And Will's gift reminds us: we can live fully now.

What About You?

For me, these challenges give purpose and help me keep finding light when darkness comes. I can only make sense of what happened by believing it is for something greater — beyond Will, beyond me. I believe Will's purpose was to give the gift of living.

He has given it to me.
He has given it to Liv.
And he offers it now to you.

So, I ask you:

What can you do to enrich your next 104 days?

Because life is short.
What's possible?

If Will's story has touched you, I'd love for you to join the Will to Liv Collective at willtoliv.com.au and keep his legacy alive in your own way.

Appendix: 104 Commitments

#lifesshortwhatspossible has become a guiding motto in my life.

Flowing forward into my new way of being is about actually LIVing all the gifts given from Will. And there have been many. His short but extraordinary life called me to step into my own in a deeper, more intentional way.

Here are my 104 commitments—one for every day of Will's life.
One for every breath he gifted me.
One for every reminder to live fully, love deeply, and keep moving forward.

1. *I WILL* be, not just do.

2. *I WILL* explore life with the curiosity and excitement Liv has.

3. *I WILL* feel and experience the joy of life.

4. *I WILL* lead the way for my daughter to a fulfilling life.

5. *I WILL* let go of control (yes, this one will be my lifelong lesson).

6. *I WILL* be open to the possibilities around me and trust that life will be okay. I want the hard slog to be replaced by ease and flow.

7. *I WILL* place my mind chatter that has consumed my life to rest.

8. *I WILL* live more from my heart—to say what I think and do what I feel.

9. *I WILL* be more open to receiving and giving love.

10. *I WILL* live connected to my purpose.

11. *I WILL* be the light that shines on others.

12. *I WILL* share Will's gift with the world and inspire others to live in a new way.

13. *I WILL* be a present and connected mum to Liv.

14. *I WILL* be more grateful for everything I have.

15. *I WILL* be more present and appreciate the moments.

16. *I WILL* understand Liv and be there for her to live her dreams and goals.

17. *I WILL* share my life with an amazing soul I am connected to on all levels.

18. *I WILL* be surrounded by prosperity and bring prosperity to everyone I meet.

19. *I WILL* do my part in Craig and I having a successful co-parenting arrangement with Liv.

20. *I WILL* approach my new life in a new way.

21. *I WILL* slow down.

22. *I WILL* focus on what is happening for me, not to me.

23. *I WILL* have fun.

24. *I WILL* be kinder to myself and others.

25. *I WILL* look for my role in situations.

26. *I WILL* believe in myself.

27. *I WILL* surround myself with amazing people.

28. *I WILL* protect my energy.

29. *I WILL* have healthy boundaries.

30. *I WILL* catch myself before I fall.

31. *I WILL* honour the gift of motherhood by being an awesome one.

32. *I WILL* be a better daughter, sister, and friend.

33. *I WILL* focus on what I can control.

34. *I WILL* be there for my friends and family.

35. *I WILL* look for the highest good in every person.

36. *I WILL* meditate regularly.

37. *I WILL* smile more at strangers.

38. *I WILL* compassionately listen.

39. *I WILL* step up and step in to situations.

40. *I WILL* speak my truth.

41. *I WILL* look for the highest intent in my emotions.

42. *I WILL* forgive more.

43. *I WILL* choose happy.

44. *I WILL* prioritise self-care.

45. *I WILL* learn from Liv.

46. *I WILL* be there for the Liv moments.

47. *I WILL* celebrate the wins.

48. *I WILL* appreciate the small things.

49. *I WILL* bring my best energy forward.

50. *I WILL* look for light in all situations.

51. *I WILL* laugh more.

52. *I WILL* listen to the whispers.

53. *I WILL* listen to my body.

54. *I WILL* connect to my intuition.

55. *I WILL* trust my intuition.

56. *I WILL* learn the lessons.

57. *I WILL* move forward with ease and flow.

58. *I WILL* surrender.

59. *I WILL* let go of expectation.

60. *I WILL* stay connected to the highest version of me.

61. *I WILL* trust in the process.

62. *I WILL* return to love.

63. *I WILL* stand up for what I believe in.

64. *I WILL* give back.

65. *I WILL* support others in need.

66. *I WILL* use my voice for good.

67. *I WILL* nourish my soul.

68. *I WILL* be me.

69. *I WILL* love me.

70. *I WILL* embrace me.

71. *I WILL* let go of expectations.

72. *I WILL* bring into my present life what I want in my future life.

73. *I WILL* honour all my feelings.

74. *I WILL* allow my feelings to move through.

75. *I WILL* travel and holiday.

76. *I WILL* speak and spread Will's message.

77. *I WILL* allow myself to be supported.

78. *I WILL* let go of fear.

79. *I WILL* allow opportunities.

80. *I WILL* look for solutions.

81. *I WILL* remember that I am and always will be enough.

82. *I WILL* live with meaning in my life.

83. *I WILL* live with graciousness in my heart.

84. *I WILL* hold space for others to be in their brilliance.

85. *I WILL* be interested in other people.

86. *I WILL* inspire.

87. *I WILL* fulfil the destined potential of my true self.

88. *I WILL* work towards flow.

89. *I WILL* know.

90. *I WILL* focus on purposeful performance.

91. *I WILL* find beauty in the mundane tasks.

92. *I WILL* allow Liv to grow into herself.

93. *I WILL* love Liv more than anything.

94. *I WILL* keep fit.

95. *I WILL* honour my body with health.

96. *I WILL* be energised.

97. *I WILL* breathe before I respond to challenging situations.

98. *I WILL* allow myself to get it wrong.

99. *I WILL* bring passion to my life and those around me.

100. *I WILL* trust.

101. *I WILL* believe.

102. *I WILL* release anger and guilt.

103. *I WILL* always connect to Will.

104. *I WILL* always love Will.

I know there will be times when I won't live up to these commitments. In fact, there will be times when I do the exact opposite. And that's okay—because we are all human, and we are all in this together.

But what I do know for sure is that I WILL always find my way back. I WILL return to my highest path. Will has ensured that for me.

I am excited for what's ahead for Liv and me in this new life. I am eternally grateful to Will for all of the gifts he has given us. He has given me—and, in turn, his little sister—the Will to Liv our most fulfilling life.

Thank you, Will.
I love you.

Acknowledgements

Writing 'Will to Liv' has reminded me just how many people walk alongside us in life. None of us get through hard times alone, and I'm grateful for every person who has been part of this journey.

Family & Friends

To my family and close friends — thank you for being there in ways big and small.

Practitioners & Guides

To the practitioners, healers, and mentors who supported me — your work helped me keep going and rebuild.

NICU

To the nurses and doctors who cared for Will with such heart. The fact that we still share moments together, even at Will's 10th birthday, says it all.

Clients & Community

To my clients and the Will to Liv community — thank you for trusting me, walking beside me, and helping carry this mission forward.

For Us All

And to everyone who has ever loved, lost, or found the 'will to liv' again — this book is for you too.

Will to Liv is a raw, powerful memoir of one mother's journey—beginning with the 104 days of her son Will's life, and continuing through the heartbreak, healing, and rebirth that followed.

But this isn't just a story about grief.
It's a story about meaning. About resilience. About choosing not just to survive—but to truly live.

It began when Angela's waters broke at just 15 weeks while on a long-awaited babymoon in Mexico—a moment that changed everything.

When her son Will was born prematurely, she entered a world of wires, beeping monitors, and whispered prayers in the NICU. For 104 days, she lived minute to minute—loving, hoping, breaking, and believing. And when Will passed away, her world cracked wide open.

This book is the legacy he left behind.

In the year after losing Will, Angela gave birth to his little sister—Liv. And in that moment, the message became clear:

You can't always choose what happens to you.
But you can choose how deeply you live.

Will. To. Liv.
Two children. One message. A mother's journey through loss and back to life—reminding us of all that:

You still have breath.
You still have choice.
And you still have the will—to truly Liv.

The Will to Liv Starts Now....

About the Author

Angela Lee is the pen name of Angela Lee Jenkins—first and foremost a mum to Will and Liv. *Will to Liv* is not just her story, but a co-creation with her son Will—whose short but powerful life inspired her to write this book—and with his little sister, Liv, who carries the message forward. Together, they remind us that love does not end; it transforms.

Alongside motherhood, Angela is a wellbeing leader and speaker with over 25 years' experience in holistic wellbeing. She blends lived wisdom with professional insight to help others reconnect with purpose, resilience, and the *'will to liv'* deeply. She is the founder of the Will to Liv collective, inspiring people to wake up and live what matters most, and she also runs Wellbeing Changemakers, a consulting practice supporting leaders to create thriving, human-centred workplaces.

Angela now lives by the ocean on the Gold Coast, Queensland, where she soaks up the everyday joys of life with her daughter, Liv.

To connect with Angela, visit **angelaleejenkins.com** or find her on Instagram at **@angelajenkins104will**.

www.ingramcontent.com/pod-product-compliance
Lightning Source LLC
Chambersburg PA
CBHW020533080526
44583CB00013B/846